LEAD NOW
or Step Aside!

Brandon,

You are a champ!

M—

p. 175

Lead NOW

or Step Aside!

The Ultimate Handbook for Student Leaders

Strategies, Advice & Ideas from America's Top Speakers, Trainers, and Authors on Youth Leadership

or Step Aside!

Compiled by
Eric Chester

Printed in the USA

Cover design and layout by Ad Graphics, Tulsa, OK

Library of Congress Catalog Card Number: 99-075966

ISBN: 0-9651447-4-7

Dedication

The sixteen co-authors of *Lead Now...or Step Aside!* dedicate this book to the incredible teachers, advisors, sponsors, and administrators who work in, with, and for the following youth organizations:

The National Association of Student Councils, DECA, FFA, FBLA, BPA, FCCLA, 4H, Key Clubs International, PRIDE, Youth to Youth, SADD, MADD, DARE, GREAT, Junior Achievement, Teen Institute, JAG, National Honor Society, FCA, NSSP, Peer Helpers Association, HOBY, and the outstanding student leadership organizations throughout Canada.

You have dedicated your time, talent, careers, and lives to the development of North America's number one resource—dynamic young leaders. We are a better people because of your continued involvement.

Acknowledgments

I would first like to thank my fifteen co-authors for their outstanding contributions to this project, *Lead Now*. I have envisioned creating this book ever since I coordinated and published our first *Teen Power* book in 1996. All of you have picked up on this vision and made it your mission and your passion. You are gifted speakers and authors, and first-rate professionals. I am lucky to have you as teammates and friends.

Special thanks to our project editor Barbara McNichol, to cover photographer Eric Weber, and to designers Jim and Barb Weems at Ad Graphics. You make putting a book like this together a snap! Thanks also to cover models (listed alphabetically) Marcos Chavez, Whitney Chester, Zac Chester, Jena Crittenden, Dillon Glathar, Nathan Havey, Patti Moon, Derek Onofrio, Dennis Phelps, Korina Selstad, David Tate, and Holly Twenhofel.

I would especially like to thank the man who is the heart and soul behind my success, Scott Thistlewaite. Scott, you are both an inspiration to me and the brother I never had.

Additional thanks go to my mentors Brent Davies, Mark Scharenbroich, Mark Sanborn, Larry Winget, Mary LoVerde, Scott Friedman, Lee Wilkerson, Ty Smith, and my father Grant Chester. You have each paved the road for me to drive on, and I am indebted to you.

Last—and certainly not least—I want to thank my best friend and incredible wife Lori for encouraging me to pursue my wild ideas. The Lord gave me the world when you came into my life, Lori, and I'll love you forever.

The Student Leader's Ultimate Handbook

Table of Contents

Part Two – Internal Wiring

Part Three – Troubleshooting

Introduction

When you think of the greatest leaders the world has ever known, what names come to mind?

Washington, Lincoln, Gandhi, Moses, M.L. King, Churchill, Roosevelt, Powell, Chavez, Anthony, Gates, Tubbman, Patton, Jordan...Among the scores of great leaders throughout history, these names are legendary. Now, what attitudes, skills, and values are common among these great leaders? What enabled them to inspire the people around them to go to unprecedented heights?

Certainly, each of these leaders will be remembered forever as **responsible** men and women of tremendous **character** who demonstrated **sportsmanship** in victory and in defeat, and **truth and honor** in every endeavor. Each was a master of **teambuilding** and knew how to develop **unity** and **influence peers** by gaining their **participation and involvement**. Instead of mere **goal setting**, they **followed through** to achieve remarkable results. Yet, none of them would have been nearly as successful if they had not possessed the **faith** to take the **risks** and **overcome adversity,** and the **creativity** to **resolve conflict** and **manage stress** when things around them turned chaotic.

As you embark on your own mission to lead, you also will be tested. There will be times when you will feel overwhelmed and under-appreciated, and you'll be forced to make sacrifices. In the end, your ability to make a L.P.D. (lasting positive difference) within your school, club, or organization will be in direct proportion to your resolve in these 16 critical areas of leadership.

The authors of this book understand the leadership challenge you have undertaken. We commend you for your courage and commitment. We know you are a *special breed*, which is why we have joined forces to bring you this *special book*.

Lead Now is not for everybody, only for those who dare to blaze new trails. In the following pages, you will find answers to your questions and questions to the answers you think you already have. You see—we're leaving nothing to chance here. We have drawn on our combined experiences working with thousands of the finest student leaders in hundreds of top youth leadership organizations to give you the best strategies, advice and ideas for leading your peers. With these tools, you'll shape your own destiny and leave your own legacy.

We know how much of a difference one individual can make when they are armed with knowledge, skills and a committed desire to make something good happen. This "ultimate handbook" will provide you with the *knowledge* and the *skills*. The *committed desire* part…well, that is on your side of the equation.

The time is now. The leadership challenge is upon you—and your peers need direction. There is absolutely no reason to wait another minute. LEAD NOW…*or Step Aside!*

Eric Chester
Co-Author, Publisher, and Project Coordinator

Part One

System Operations

chapter 1

Creativity

By C. Kevin Wanzer

Grow Up to Be a Child

LEAD NOW
or Step Aside!

Creativity

By C. Kevin Wanzer

Grow Up to Be a Child

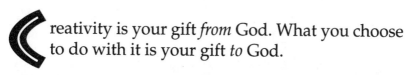 reativity is your gift *from* God. What you choose to do with it is your gift *to* God.

It is not possible to complete this chapter wrong ... unless, of course, you rip out the pages and eat them in front of your classmates while howling at the bright incandescent lights that shine in your glorious class-room. That would be completing this chapter wrong. However, you would get your recommended daily allowance of fiber ... and ink.

First things first.

"In the beginning, God *created* ... "

There you have it. I would say God is a pretty effective leader. And since He started with creativity, why shouldn't you?

I used to think the verse was, "In the beginning, God created Kevin and Earth." As a kid, I was so flattered and excited that God created *me* before anything else. Later, I realized the correct verbiage was, "In the beginning, God created *heaven* and Earth." Oh, well. Close enough.

Creativity is like that, too … close enough is many times good enough. Just the process of using your creativity breeds success. There is no wrong way to be creative. Creativity is authenticity. And there is no wrong way to be authentic. Creativity is the recess of life, the dessert of leadership.

This book allows you to enjoy your dessert first.

You are You-nique

You represent the majority of one. Congratulations. You will always win in determining how *you* feel. You are *You-nique* You are creative. You were born that way. It makes sense to regress to the simple things of life that breed creativity.

Give yourself permission to be authentic and the opportunity to rediscover who you truly are. Your goal is to chip away the shell that surrounds the creative child who longs to run and play and laugh and sing.

Over time, your creativity may get stifled and drown in the sea of self-doubt. "I can't paint. I can't think of anything different. I am no good at being creative. Imagination and creativity are for children."

You are right. Creativity *is* for children. If you were born into this world … and most of us were … then you have parents. If you have parents, then you are a child. Therefore, by your own admission, you are a creative child.

Remember how wonderful it felt to chase butterflies through the backyard … to make forts out of couch cushions … to finger paint … to toe paint … to paint your kitty cat ... to make forts out of your painted cat's toes ... to laugh so hard you shoot milk through your nose ... to hold the hand of your friend for no reason at all ... to make your own world out of an empty refrigerator box ... to squeeze your mom with the biggest hug in the whole wide world.

The world was wonderful and it was everything you wanted it to be.

Then came the first day of school. And with it came the rules.

Don't scribble. Stay inside the lines. Paint by numbers. The sky must be blue. The grass must be green. Don't lick the cat. Sit up straight. Don't sing that silly song you made up. Sing this song that is already written. No dessert unless you eat all your vegetables. Stop making a mountain out of your mashed potatoes.

Why?

Slowly, the creative spirit within starts to hibernate. Waiting ever so patiently in the corner. Longing for you to call to it. To invite it to come out and play.

Truth is, life was simple then. Truth is, life is simple now.

That is, if you choose it to be. You see, life is only as difficult as you perceive it.

When you were a kid, even work was fun. My mom used to have us play the game "Who can clean his room the quickest?" We used to scurry around and, within an hour, we cleaned our rooms immaculately. The closet was really packed, but our rooms were clean. Work can be play with the right attitude. Therefore, you don't get homework assignments; you get *homeplay* assignments.

Create Your Own *Creative Journal*

You will need a creative journal to get the most out of this. Anything will do. But get creative. Find a journal that represents *you*. Or make your own.

There are five key creative homeplay assignments to help you on your journey. I know not everyone will do everything. Pick and choose. Do what you like. Give yourself permission to be silly. To be a kid. Heck, write out a permission slip that allows you to be who you are. Sign it in crayon and keep it with you. If people ask, "Who told you that you could be so crazy?" take out your slip and show them.

The only rule: have fun with the homeplay assignments. I double dare you to take off your water wings, let your walls down, and dive in headfirst. Just remember, you cannot do anything wrong. Each homeplay assignment will help you uncover at the creative kid who can continue to lead you to be the authentic, creative leader that you are. Enjoy the ride.

Homeplay Assignment #1: Defining Your Creative Kid.

"Children are the bearers of life in its simplest form. Children are color blind and still free from the complications, greed and hatred that will slowly be instilled on them in life."
– Keith Haring

Grab your creative journal. Think of all the magical words that help describe your creative essence. Words that make you glad you exist. Words that capture your creative essence. Use these words to get you going ... or pick your own ... or *even make up your own new words* that define you.

Rare ... Gifted ... Magical ... Authentic ... Hilarious ... Wild ... Energized ... Spiritual ... Angelic ... Unusual ... Truthful ... Courageous ... Fair ... Imaginative ... Confident ... Kind ... Empathetic ... Sincere ... Forgiving ... Loyal ... Cooperative ... Giving ... Compassionate ... Responsible ...

Decorate the cover of your creative journal with those words. Now, choose one word that really captures you today. Grab some markers, construction paper, and write that word as creatively as you want. Tape that paper on the ceiling above your bed so you can see it lying down. Change that word whenever you would like. That word can help awaken your creative spirit when you wake each day.

Homeplay Assignment #2: Write Now Right Now!

"I want to go on living even after my death! And therefore I am grateful to God for giving me this gift, the possibility of developing myself, and of writing, of expressing all that is within me."
– Anne Frank

Your creative journal can be one of the most powerful gifts you have ever given yourself. Use it as a way to communicate to the creative kid within.

I began keeping a creative journal quite some time ago. It is a wonderful way to "keep tabs" on my creative kid and allow him to talk to me. It is amazing how much help you can be to yourself if you just sit still and listen.

Consider writing each day, if you can, just stream of consciousness. Put the pen on the paper and keep writing. Keep going for ten minutes straight. If you cannot think of anything, just write, "I can't think of a thing." Once you break through and keep writing, you will be amazed with the results.

Here are some ideas to light that creative-writing spark:

- Each day, record a moment of the day. A simple event that touched your creative heart that you want to capture.

- A funny or bizarre quotation you may have heard in a conversation. I once overheard someone actually say, "It is wrong to pistol whip your tailor." Never could I have imagined hearing those words uttered by another human. I had to write it down.

- Write a fan letter to yourself. Sign it, *"from a secret admirer. "* Mail it.

- Write a letter to your creative kid with your less dominant hand. Use a crayon.

- Write a letter to your favorite schoolteacher and let him or her know what he or she meant to you.

- Write a letter you have always wanted to write but couldn't find the courage to do it.

- List three things for which you are truly thankful.

Most important, ask yourself, "What do I want?"

That question is simple enough ... so go for it ... what do *you* want? What is *one* creative idea or goal you would like to pursue?

What prohibits you from reaching that goal? List *everything*! Remember, you already are a creative star...you just need to let yourself shine.

What is one step you can take to get to that goal? Just one tiny step. Write it down and then create a deadline by which you will have it finished.

Congratulations. You are one step closer to the goal you dreamed about.

Now, flip back to that page with all the reasons you are not able to conquer your creative dream. Burn it (unless, of course, you are in school). Or just rip it into tiny confetti and toss it in the trash so those reasons are now gone. You have ~~work~~ fun to do.

Homeplay Assignment #3: Take Yourself on a Creative Recess.

> *"He who knows others is learned.*
> *He who knows himself is wise."*
> *– Lao-tse*

"You! Party of One."

Remember the highlight of your elementary school day? Recess!

Take yourself on a creative recess, by yourself, once a week. C'mon ... give it a try. Plan something special you would like to do by yourself. Plan it as if someone very special is coming along.

Check out a movie you have been waiting to see. Take a run in a wooded park. Have a picnic overlooking the water. Or go to that museum you have driven past for years, but never visited. Whatever it is, plan it and do it ... and do not dare think of asking someone else to tag along.

Being alone can be a positive tool in rediscovering your creative kid. After all, when you are young, you are usually all alone when your imagination runs wild.

Homeplay Assignment #4: Be Quiet and Talk.

"God is the friend of silence. Trees, flowers, and grass grow in silence. Notice how the sun, moon and stars move in silence."
– Mother Teresa

Take some time to be still and talk to yourself. Yep, you heard me right ... or you read me right. Talk to yourself. If you are able to look in a mirror and see a person you are happy to look up to as a role model, you have it made. (Unless, of course, you look in the mirror and see a man with a ski mask standing behind you. In that case, put down this book and run. No, wait a second. Pick the book back up. Turn around and throw the book at the man and then run. But don't forget your journal.)

Take a moment each week to checkup with yourself. Stand in front of a mirror and just say the things you need to say. You really do have someone who wants you to succeed and be the creative person you are.

It is amazing what we can hear when we listen to the silence.

When most people are young, they live and thrive creatively. They enjoy the simple things of life: daydreaming, butterfly-watching, or rolling down a hill in the tall cool grass. Simplicity is the comfortable silence of being alive. The lucky ones are surrounded by adults who reinforce and celebrate the power and glory of youth and creativity. Some people are not so lucky. Their creativity is compromised and slowly it disappears. They then fall asleep and lose their creative essence. I challenge you to wake up. Notice the simple things in life. What are they?

This is your wake-up call for the rest of your life ... so you can continue to be your own role model.

Homeplay Assignment #5: Create An Imagi-NATION in Your School.

"Imagination is more important then knowledge."
– Albert Einstein

Creativity and imagination go hand in hand. It is impossible to have one without the other.

Simply put, creativity results from using your imagination. Without a good imagination, it is difficult to be productively creative and willing to change.

In Hawaii, there is a philosophy that believes there are no adults, just different ages and levels of childhood. So as you age, you do not become an old person, just a really big kid. (That probably explains why Hawaiians consume more SPAM then any other state in the country. But I digress ...)

Imagine if you lived with the idea that, as you age, your creativity, love, and imagination only increase. You become more tolerant and empathetic toward others. You dare to take more risks ... to laugh at the silliest things.

What if your school were like that? It can be.

What if there were an imagi-NATION? A place where there were no silly or bad ideas? A place where the grass could be purple and the sky could always be a rainbow? Although a nation like this may likely never exist, you have the power to bring it into the halls of your schools. Use your imagination to create a school of imagi-NATION. A place that celebrates the spirit of creativity and being young.

List all the things you wish were true about your school and its atmosphere. Create a dream list, then take tiny steps toward achieving just one of those goals. Even if you are not able to accomplish all you want this year, you still open doors for others to follow in your footsteps.

The sky is the limit.

Reach for the sky...not the ceiling

"I wonder how many birds die in cages,
thinking the ceiling is the sky?"
– Og Mandino

Everyone is creative is some way. The key is discovering how your creativity is best suited for you. Whether it is art, writing, running, planning a special evening, cooking, or talking to others, creativity is simply whatever you do with what you imagine. If you can imagine, you can create.

If you remember the life lessons of childhood, you will realize that life is simple.

If you want to be happier in life ... then be happier.
If you want to be friendlier ... be friendlier.
If you want to enjoy life more ... enjoy life more.
If you want to be more creative ... be creative.
I know it may sound simplistic.
It is.

And so is the rest of the chapter. Now you have enjoyed your luscious creative dessert, dive into the meat of it all. But keep a little treat on the side. Feel free to come back and tackle a homeplay assignment or two. The more you allow yourself to be creative, the more effectively and authentically you will lead.

Life is about moments. Relish them. Look into the eyes of the people you love— really take time to look and see them. Memorize the feeling of a loved one's embrace. Squeeze them for just a second longer, for in the long run, those seconds will last for an eternity. Create moments. Collect moments. Relish life, creatively.

Creative Spirits

Life is the essence of creativity. Each person's soul is a product of divine creativity. By nature, we are all creative spirits. Whether or not people choose to act on their creative gifts or disregard them is totally an individual choice...there is no "teaching" someone to be creative. You already are. Like breathing. From the moment you were born. You continue breathing to keep your body alive. And if you stopped breathing, you would die. There would not be chapters in leadership books about the importance of oxygen because, by the time people realize they stopped breathing, it might be too late.

The same goes with creativity. By the time you believe you have lost it, you may feel it is too late to recapture it. You may make excuses as to why you are not creative like, "it's is for weird people or little kids." You go through the motions of life ... looking into the creative worlds of others, secretly longing and wondering what happened, and praying for your own creative kid to someday shine.

Truth is, you can always regain your creative kid. Always. It is never too late. Never, never, never. This chapter gives you permission to allow your creative light to shine and for you to grow up.

Grow up to be a child.

Questions, Activities & Exercises

Creativity Discussion Enticers

1. Create up five words and definitions you wish were in the dictionary that could help the world.

2. Select five words from the dictionary that you hope someday might be eliminated because they no longer have meaning.

3. Discuss three movies, books and people that make you: LAUGH, THINK and FEEL. Why do they have such an impact on your life?

4. Create a list of ten things you miss about being a little kid. Select one of those things and do it today.

5. Create your own certificate of authenticity. Get as creative as you want. On it, consider including:

   • A statement or quotation by you that you want the world to hear

   • A list of people you consider role models

   • A person who looks up to you as a role model

   • Words that you are happy exist (For example, laughter, enlightenment, passion ...)

6. If your class were the United States Government, what are three creative laws you would pass to help make the world a better, loving, enlightened place to live?

7. Begin your life to-do list…a list of ten creative things you would love to do in this lifetime. Set a time line for at least one of them and just do it.

8. Create a wall of fame…a wall that celebrates the people in this world who you admire and help make you a positive person.

9. Create a list of five people, living, you would like to invite to dinner. Who would they be and why? Write letters to them explaining what they mean to you and why. Invite them to dinner. Find out their addresses and, what the heck, put a stamp on the envelopes and seal them. Then, without thinking about it, drop them in the mailbox. You might be surprised by who responds.

10. Write a letter or card to yourself and date it one year from today. Say everything you want to say about how proud you are of yourself and how far you have come. Put it in an envelope with your name and address along with a nifty stamp. Then place the envelope in a larger one and send it off to me. I will hold onto the card and return it to you at the beginning of the next year.

About C. Kevin Wanzer

Kevin attended assemblies in the 10th grade...as the speaker. Since then, he has been on a life long journey of compassion and loving kindness towards young people and those who impact the lives of young people. With each presentation, Kevin is able to share his hilarious insights about life, leadership, love and living authentically. If you have not experienced Kevin yourself, make sure to put it on your life's to-do list. Kevin lives in Indianapolis, and spends his free time painting, writing, running and sharing special moments with his canine soul companion, Dreifus. Visit Kevin on the World Wide Web for more great creativity homeplay assignments.

Just Say Ha!
P.O. Box 30384, Indianapolis, IN 46230-0384
317-253-4242   fax 317-475-0956   Toll Free: 1-800-4-KEVIN-W
Email: LeadNow@KevinWanzer.com • Web Site: www.KevinWanzer.com

chapter 2

Goal Setting

By Jennifer Esperante Gunter

Goal Setting:
The Map for Goal Getting!

LEAD NOW
or Step Aside!

Goal Setting

By Jennifer Esperante Gunter

Goal Setting:
The Map for Goal Getting!

When I was 14 years old, a speaker shared this valuable lesson with me: *"When a ship leaves London en route to New York, it doesn't pull out of the harbor without a charted course and an estimated time of arrival. The captain knows exactly where and how far to go every day to reach the destination."*

As the captain of your own ship, achieving your goals requires knowing both *what* you want and *how* you plan to get it. This is the *goal-setting* skill.

As a speaker, I travel often. When I check in at the airport, the first question they ask is, *"Final destination?"* What would happen if I answered, *"Uhhh... I dunno!"* They would look at me like I was insane! Like I was joking! Why? Because every person that gets on an airplane *must* have a destination. Well, the same goes for you. *You* must have a destination, an end in sight, a goal to ever get anywhere.

That's actually the easy part. The challenge begins with *planning* how to get there. If you were planning a trip to Disneyland, you'd need to buy a map, choose the roads to take, decide where to stay, and find out about the places you might visit along the way. Once you start driving, you may get lost, tired, or hungry, and face traffic jams, closed roads, and detours as you go. Yes, they will slow you down, but it all becomes worth it when you and your traveling companions finally stop the car and yell, *"We're heeeeee-ere!"*

Well, just as you would never embark on a trip without a map, train schedule, airline ticket, or bus fare—you should never set out for your goal without a *PLAN!*

In my experience, most people who fail to achieve their goals are those that begin their journey with just an *idea* instead of a plan. Instead of mapping things out ahead of time, they choose to figure out the plan as they go. Imagine how long it would take you to get from Kansas to Disneyland if you decided to get in the car one day without any planning. You could get lost and have to ask for directions, run out of gas, find out you didn't have enough money, get lost and have to stop for directions again, and arrive to find all the local hotels booked! You'd be stuck with a suitcase and nowhere to go. *BUMMER!*

Yes, you would still reach your destination (although days behind schedule and probably frustrated), but planning ahead would have eliminated all that stress, lost time, and confusion. Just as with the Disneyland trip, lack of planning always makes it take longer to achieve your goal.

Few journeys to reach a goal are easy. But, with planning, your path can be easier! Whether you have a personal or team goal, the following six steps are for you. Read them. Apply them. Master them. They will bring you amazing results!

1. Write It! — The Goal and Your Deadline

Once you've determined what it is you want, *write it down*—both *what* you want and *when* you want it. Setting a deadline for your goal will help you understand just how much time you have to make this thing work. Then put signs that state your goal on your bathroom mirror, car dashboard, the refrigerator, your closet door—several places you will see every day so you're constantly reminded of your goals. These signs will keep you *focused* and *inspired*.

For example:

"Jeff Roxas is the 2004-2005 Student Body President!"

"On March 15, 2004, the Class of 2004 has $3000 in our bank account!"

"On April 17, 2003, Natalia Reese wins 1st place in Free-Style Swimming at the regional swim meet!"

Notice that these goals are written in the *present tense* and are *very specific*! You can't just say: *"Jeff Roxas will be president."* This doesn't say *when* you'll be president nor does it state that it actually happened. It only describes it possibly happening... some day!

Read your goal out loud every day. It will become more and more believable to you, helping you to stay *motivated* and *confident*.

2. Tell Everyone about It!

Another way to stay focused and motivated is to tell people who love you (such as your friends and family) about your goals. Explain *what* you are working toward and *when* you plan on achieving it, and they'll become your cheerleaders. These cheerleaders will ask, "How's it going?" and give you support, often motivating you more than you expect.

My roommate in college, Stacey, cheered me on toward acquiring scholarship money I needed to pay tuition. She helped me stay focused by keeping on me about my deadlines. She even created a calendar that showed my deadlines toward my goal, and would place a sticker on the day when I accomplished them. Yes, it was silly. But every time I walked to the bathroom, kitchen, etc., I would see this calendar hanging on the hall wall and remember how much I still had to do. Then...well, I would do it.

Who in *your* life might do the same for you? Tell them about your goal and you won't have to set out on your journey alone. Even if this is a team goal, there are people outside your team who can help. Find them. Tell them. And let them cheer *you* on, too!

3. Draw It! — The Map to Your Goal

Now that you have a written goal, a deadline, and a cheering section, it's time to make a plan to achieve your goal. A plan can be as simple as listing all the necessary action steps and checking them off as you do each one. Or, you can draw a *Goal Map*. Here's how:

- First, identify the three largest, most general steps needed to reach the goal. For example, if the goal is: *"Attend NYU and graduate in the spring of 2005,"* your three largest steps might be: *"1. Find money 2. Get good grades 3. Apply."* Write your goal at the top of a large sheet of paper. Underneath it, list your three general steps from left to right.

- Next, under each of the three general steps, write the three most important specific steps it would take to complete it. Under *"1. Find money"* for example, you might write *"a. Get scholarships b. Get loans c. Get a job."*

- If you find that any of your specific steps are still too big to tackle all at once, break them down further. You know, write three *smaller* steps it would take to complete each specific step. For example, *"a. Get scholarships"* might require: *"1) Research scholarships 2) Get reference letters 3) Fill out applications"* etc. Keep expanding your map until it includes all the steps you need. Get my drift?

Setting Goals for School Events

Here is a *real* example. A student council team in my community needed to raise money for their school events. Someone came up with the idea of Mr. GQ: an evening fashion show/pageant where high school boys modeled and competed in evening wear, swimsuits, talent, and on-stage questions. Not only was it a lot of fun, but it was so unique that people from all over the community attended. How could they resist such a crazy event?

Sponsors donated money, tuxedo shops donated tuxes, surf shops loaned swimwear and surfboards, and people who didn't even have teenagers going to the school paid $7 to watch the show. High school girls acted as their escorts and local community leaders volunteered as judges.

That first year, they raised *over* $2000! They reached their goal! The following year, they promoted the event via newspapers, radio, and posters at local stores. They sold more than 600 tickets and raised over $4500! It was such a success (and a riot!) that they now continue this "tradition" every year.

Here is how their *Goal Map* started:

GOAL: Raise $2000
HOW: Mr. GQ Fashion Show
WHEN: October 16, 1997
WHERE: High School Gymnasium

1. Get sponsors	2. Find guys to enter	3. Get an audience
a. Ask local businesses for $$.	a. Advertise in school announcements/ bulletins	a. Decide ticket price
b. Decide what they get in return (name in program, advertisement, free tickets?)	b. Ask guys we know. (Be sure to include a good cross-section of school population; maybe have a rep from each club, grade and/or cultural group)	b. Post signs at high traffic stores
c. Ask local stores for tangible donations: tuxes, sodas, maybe their time (e.g., a DJ, judges, etc.)	c. Determine how many guys we need	c. Invite people via a community mailing and tell EVERYONE we know!!

As you can see from their *Goal Map*, it already looks like a lot of work and yet this was only the beginning!

To continue their Map, they needed to break it down more and more, i.e., listing three *specific* businesses they would ask for money, decide ten *specific* guys they would invite to join, etc. After a thorough process of planning, they had an incredibly detailed map of *how* to reach their goal of $2000. By breaking it down, being specific, and creating the plan, they also saw exactly how much work the goal required them to do.

A detailed plan gives you a *reality check* about what you head out to do and tests if you are committed to doing the work. If it seems like too much, you can alter the goal or scale back the plan. But, thank goodness you figured it out before you got in the car and wasted all that gas! Right?

4. Schedule It!

If this is a team goal, then it's time to delegate *who* will take on what responsibilities and *when* their deadlines will be. If your goal is a personal goal, then you have to do all the work, step by step by step. Like Stacey did for me, you should create a calendar that shows all the deadlines for your goal to keep you on track. With a team, give each person a copy so everyone can see exactly *what* is due *when* and from *whom*. Your calendar will eliminate confusion, miscommunication, and possible failure. It's also another tactic for motivation to get it all done!

5. Just Do It!

Once you've got the map and schedule, it's time to take the dive. In other words, it's time to do the work you said you were going to do! If you find that you're not moving forward, don't just flake out—*find help!* Get a buddy like my friend Stacey to cheer you along, or trade your job with someone else on your team who'd be better at it. Don't make excuses. Get up! Get going! And *do the WORK*!

6. Stay Positive

The worst thing anyone can do is give up. Understand ahead of time that achieving your goal could involve a lot of work. When challenges appear, stay positive! Use positive self-talk. Tell yourself and your teammates things like: "Come on, you can do this!" or "Go for it!" Then, *see* yourself actually getting it done, achieving your goal, and enjoying the rewards at the end! See yourself at the finish line, winning the gold medal. See your team celebrating the successful event! After all, your mind is like a big TV screen. What you see is what most likely will transpire.

Remember, every morning when you rise out of bed—teeth unbrushed and hair sticking up—your attitude is as much a choice for you as what you'll have for breakfast and what you'll wear to work or school. Life is about choices, and the quality of your life depends on the quality of your decisions. Your attitude might just be the most important decision of all. So choose to be positive and strive to do so everyday!

Are You Ready to Take Action?

Even though I am an international speaker and author, I certainly didn't start with all of the answers, nor do I assume I have them all now. Believe me, I had many challenges and often got lost and frustrated along *my* way. But the bottom line is, to get where I am today, I did what I have told you to do in this chapter. I decided what I wanted, took the necessary steps towards my goal, and after many challenges and mistakes, today I'm living my dreams.

If you follow the simple steps in this chapter, I know you will do the same. So, come on. Don't just sit there. *Get up! Get focused! Get to work!* Yes, start *goal setting* and you'll be *goal getting* before you know it.

Questions, Activities & Exercises

Create Your Own Goal-Setting Map Right Now

What is *your* goal?

Write it down and *be specific.* Don't say, *"To get a job."* Say instead, *"To be a full-time practicing physician on the Pediatric Floor at Memorial Hospital."* See the difference? So what if it changes along your way. Write it down anyway! The key is to know *exactly* what you want to accomplish right now. *Now, write yours here.*

   My / Our Goal is:

When do you want to achieve it?

You must have a *deadline*! Without one, you have nothing to go by. And, don't say, *"8 years,"* because eight years from now you'll still think you have 8 years! Write down *"June 2004."* Be *specific*! *Now, write yours here.*

My / Our Deadline is:

Put the two together and post it where you can see it every day.

For example: *"It's April 16, 2004 and Bob Richmond is President of the Senior Class!"* or *"It's Oct. 15, 2005, and our Homecoming Dance is a smashing success! We raised the needed $1000!" Now write yours here.*

Who will be your cheerleaders?

List them here.

Create your *Goal Map*—the plan that will lead you to your goal.

Step #1	Step #2	Step #3
a)	a)	a)
1)	1)	1)
2)	2)	2)
b)	b)	b)
1)	1)	1)
2)	2)	2)
c)	c)	c)
1)	1)	1)
2)	2)	2)

Draft a calendar with deadlines for the steps above. Then put these dates on a master calendar for everyone to see.

What are some phrases you can say to yourself or your team that will keep you positive?

For example: *"You are really good at this,"* or *"26 more days. We're almost there!" Now write yours here.*

What are some winning pictures you can imagine?

For example: *"I see myself standing on the platform with the 1st place trophy,"* or *"Our Red Ribbon Week Assembly is a success! Every student is dressed in red and committed to our Pledge!" Now, write yours here.*

About Jennifer Esperante Gunter

Jennifer (aka **The Cha Cha Queen**) brings high-energy, charisma, and a life-changing message to audiences across America & Internationally. A Keynote Speaker, Workshop Leader, and Mistress of Ceremonies since 1989, she has entertained audiences from twenty to 5000. Why do countless letters, e-mails, and calls pour in after Jennifer speaks?? Her Message is Powerful. Her Personality is Unforgettable. *She Loves Youth!* Miss Sonoma County 1992. Miss San Francisco 1993. Has produced shows for the San Francisco 49ers & Miss America Program. Holds a degree in Psychology. Author of *Winning with the Right Attitude.* Co-author of TEEN POWER and PreTEEN POWER!

Jennifer Esperante Gunter
P.O. Box 8368, Santa Rosa, CA. 95407
707-523-7004   fax 707-523-7047   Toll Free: 800-357-6112
Email: jennifer@chaqueen.com • Web Site: www.chaqueen.com

chapter 3

Influencing Peers

By Craig Hillier

A Gentle Pull Works Better than a Hard Push!

LEAD NOW
or Step Aside!

Influencing Peers

By Craig Hillier

A Gentle Pull Works Better than a Hard Push!

She saw seniors urinate on underclassmen, break bottles over heads, throw eggs on faces, pour vinegar in eyes, and toss green hair dye on student's heads. Nikki stood up and said high school hazing had gone too far. She convinced the school administration to create new policies and punishments for those responsible for the terrible treatment. Then she went to work on the state government. Two years later, the Minnesota legislature named an anti-hazing bill after her. Nikki helped change the state.

Craig sees a 10-year-old boy sold as slave labor in a third world country and becomes outraged. He visits the country and eventually meets with world leaders. Then he creates a non-profit organization with thousands of members, all under the age of 18, promoting an end to child labor. The organization has persuaded hundreds of companies to end their relationships with vendors who employ children as their workers. Craig helped change the world.

The gym was jamming. Music was blaring. The 900 students were rowdy anticipating the assembly. As the music faded, Jennifer took the microphone to introduce the guest speaker. The students stopped talking to give her their undivided attention. Thank goodness. I was the speaker! Jennifer helped change her school.

Each of these real-life young leaders has an essential quality. . . **INFLUENCE.**

Without influence, it's impossible to lead.

With it, you can change people, change perspectives, and change the world— *at least your corner of it!*

Webster's dictionary defines influence as "the act or power of producing an effect without apparent force or direct authority." In addition, it's the ability to make something happen without intimidation or threats. People are *pulled* onto a team because they are inspired, not because they are afraid of being *pushed around* or humiliated. People who lead by positive influence are those who walk into a room and brighten it by their presence. People with negative influence brighten the room by leaving it.

The question is, how can YOU develop influence?

Before diving into the keys to accomplish this, let's look at what factors influence most teams.

Peers are major influences. You see friends with new hairstyles, clothes, or cool shoes. The next thing you know, *their* styles become *your* style.

The **media** is also a strong influence. Creative advertisements are easily recalled in your mind. Phrases or actions from a movie or TV program get repeated in the hallway.

Parents play a role in our thinking. Because you've been around them so long, their words, actions, and beliefs have become a part of you.

You influence you. As a young person, you have the ability to decide which trends, thoughts, and actions you're going to buy into and which ones you leave behind.

Good or bad, you know that peers, parents, and the media shape your thinking.

Creating influence with others is not an easy task, but it can be learned. There are no guarantees. However, if you will use the following ideas, you will become someone others *willingly* follow.

Create a vision

When I was a little kid, a view master was one of my favorite toys. For those who are too young to remember this great toy, it resembles a pair of binoculars. A disk that has photographic or cartoon-like pictures is placed in the view master. When I looked through the viewer, each picture on the disk appeared larger than life. I would flip the lever to move the disk to the next picture. When viewed in sequence, the pictures created a story. The absence of words forced me to use my imagination to develop my own story line.

Some Iowa students had a new vision for their school, which was very old and run down. The hallways were dark and dingy; the bathrooms were beat up and dirty. So the students created a vision of what the school could look like. They designed a few sketches of wall murals on paper and approached the principal about their ideas to paint them. He immediately gave them the authority to make the changes. The leaders enlisted the help of other students and they started to work on "operation face lift." Of course, the building is still old but it now looks a lot better because of their work. Just like looking through a view master, the students first saw the murals in their minds, then literally made them appear larger than life on the school walls.

Influence insight: When you are trying to influence, explain the big-picture end result *first*.

Center on others

This reflects an ancient principle. People don't care how much you know until they know how much you care. If you really want to gain influence with others, work in their best interest. Only pretending to be concerned about others seldom works in your favor. You may know people who try to trick others into believing they care, but it's easy to see they are only concerned about themselves. This relates to a formula I share in my leadership course, the C.A.R.E. formula.

C = Compliment three people each day. Make sure the compliment is sincere. Instead of being jealous or thinking a compliment won't matter, challenge yourself to share your thoughts. You will be amazed at how people respond when you make comments positively.

A = Act in others' best interests. Think with compassion about students in your school who are either new or don't have a lot of positive things happening in their lives. Do you have a minute to talk with these students despite the possibility your friends will wonder what you're doing? If you have the compassion to do so, people respect the courage it takes to get out of your comfort zone to make others comfortable.

R = Respect the differences in others. It's so easy to walk on campus and immediately judge others by external appearances. Too often, these judgments are way off. It's much better to reserve judgment until you have a more understanding of others.

E = Extend a helping hand. Your school, church and community need you. Nothing shows you care more than getting involved by willingly giving your time and energy.

This formula works! I received a letter from a young man in the Minneapolis area who heard this idea at a leadership seminar at his school. I gave all of the students a C.A.R.E. commitment card as they exited the session, and he taped his card inside his locker. Every day, he repeated his commitment to this formula. The following year, he was elected student body president representing 2000 students. According to the note he sent me, using the principle on a daily basis was a major factor in his victory.

Influence insight: If people know you truly care, they trust you. If they trust you, you can influence them.

Be open to feedback

Have you ever seen yourself on videotape and thought, "Do I really look like that when I make that face?" Or have you ever heard your own voice on audiotape and thought, "There's no way that's me. I don't sound like that!" Guess what? You do. It's a form of feedback.

Blaine Lee, author of the *Power Principle*, says, "In order to be an influence, you must be willing to be influenced."

People who get defensive when someone gives them a suggestion usually feel insecure about their abilities. However, leaders who openly ask for feedback from their friends, teachers, coaches, or parents demonstrate confidence. These leaders understand no one is perfect or has all the answers. When you ask people for their input, they feel their opinion counts. Many times, others will share ideas that you may not have thought of on your own.

Top-notch schools ask for their students' feedback on issues ranging from lunch menus to improving pep rallies. As a leader, you can gain trust by pursuing feedback from others. Please remember, receiving feedback can be flattering or flattening. If you receive some negative feedback, learn from it and don't let it get you down. Use the information as a step up, not as a setback.

Keys to asking for feedback on your performance or about a new vision/idea:

- Ask someone who cares about the situation.
- Ask specific questions.
- Ask more than one person or group.
- Ask someone with experience.
- Listen with an open mind.

Influence insight: Feedback is the breakfast of champions.

Walk the talk

Unfortunately, some people believe that, in order to lead, you must be loud. Brash, obnoxious comments and gestures seldom create leadership and influence. Too many people are talking loudly in our schools but not saying anything of value.

A perfect example of someone who "walked the talk" was Mother Teresa. She was definitely not a loud leader. Mother Teresa was a humble leader with incredible influence. Every day, she fed and served the poor.

A question I often ask in my sessions is, "If Mother Teresa were still alive and she approached you and asked for your help for 10 days, would you be able to turn her down?" I have asked this question to thousands of students and no one has ever answered yes. She wasn't loud; she simply walked her talk.

If you lead a group and are consistently the last to arrive and first to leave, there is a problem. If you constantly question your advisor's decisions behind his or her back, don't be surprised if your peers do the same with you. People watch your effort and attitude. If you are in extra curricular activities, your teammates watch how you respond to a bad call by an official or judge. If you stomp your feet in disgust, it's difficult to tell another teammate to calm down given the same set of circumstances.

Walking the talk essentially means you set the tone you want by your words, actions, and attitude. **You can't get what you're not willing to give first**. Asking others to do something you can't or won't do isn't going to work. Say, "*Let's* go make it happen" and not "*You* go make it happen."

Influence insight: Influence is not measured by how loud your *voice* is but how loudly your *actions* speak.

Complete the task

It's not enough just to get started on an idea or project. It must come to a conclusion. To have influence with others, develop a track record for finishing the job ... something as simple as cleaning up after an event or collecting all the prizes from local merchants for a fundraiser proves you can deliver. If you promise to make a change, live up to your word.

I read a newspaper article about a principal in a Pennsylvania school who continually challenged the students to "stick to it" and follow through on their commitments. The students got the message and decided to use the "stick to it" theme to their advantage. They sold pieces of duct tape to students and staff. After raising several hundred dollars, they taped the principal to the cafeteria wall. Of course, he was a willing participant. The money they raised went into a scholarship fund.

As a student leader, it's easy to overcommit your time and energy. Overcommitment leads to frustration and stress. If you feel stressed, following through becomes a challenge. It's usually better to say "yes" to the things you know you can follow through on rather than saying "yes" to everything and only following through occasionally. Leaders who consistently use the power of completion radiate personal confidence.

Influence insight: When you follow through on your commitments and show a "stick-to-it" attitude, you build credibility. Credibility creates change.

Develop people power

Skilled leaders understand how to work with people. They know how to draw others in and create enthusiasm. Great influencers know how to develop magical words that turn a person from a "no-way" attitude to a "I'll give it a try" mentality.

The following five strategies will help you create people power.

1. Treat each person as a "10." John Maxwell, author of *Developing the Leader Within You*, challenges leaders to assume everyone they come in contact with has an imaginary "10" written on their forehead. Understand that everyone, and I mean everyone, wants to be treated as a "10"—the best! No one wants to be looked down at or demeaned regardless of the situation. If you are thrilled when certain people arrive and sad when they depart, you send a powerful message about how you feel about their presence.

2. Use people's names. It's been said the sweetest words in the world are "thank you" and a person's name. Whether you've known someone for years or have just been introduced, using names creates a bond. You may be surprised at how well people respond when you include their names in conversation. It's not uncommon to get a larger portion and better service at a restaurant when addressing the server by name. Occasionally, I've been upgraded to a first class seat from coach on an airplane just by using the gate agent's name and being congenial. This simple skill is very effective.

3. Give people a break when they make a mistake. Everyone makes mistakes. When others goof up and you are on receiving end of their blunders, be gentle with them. This does two things. First, it demonstrates you understand no one is perfect. Second, it sets the tone when you make a mistake. If you blow up when someone else messes up, get ready, because the same response is coming your way when *you* mess up.

4. Show your passion. People admire those who are fired up by a great cause. I can still remember high school teachers who had a sincere passion for their subjects. Their passion sparked enthusiasm in the students they taught. Don't be afraid to get fired up about what you do.

5. Plant the seeds of time. It's nearly impossible to influence from a distance. To gain influence, stay "in the trenches" working with your teammates. The more time you invest with them, the better you know them. The seeds of time spent with people eventually sprout into an awesome team.

Influence insight: Mastering "people power" skills creates the winning edge.

Influencing is a powerful skill that can be learned. It takes practice and time. If you're willing to go the extra mile and consistently use the ideas presented in this chapter, you'll be amazed at the results! You'll draw people to you like a magnet. And a magnetized group of leaders creates a strong, positive voice that others in their school, church and community will *want* to follow.

Questions, Activities & Exercises

1. Who has had the biggest influence in your life? Why?

2. As you look at what you are wearing today, discuss why you initially purchased the items. What or who influenced the decisions?

3. Discuss examples of people who have used their influence in a positive and negative way.

4. Write down three places you are going to use people's name where you normally don't. This should happen within the next four days.

   1.

   2.

   3.

What were the results?

5. Write down the C.A.R.E. formula on a piece of paper and place it in a spot where you will see every day. Use the formula and observe its impact.

6. Just for the fun of it, start a new fad or trend. Sit at a different table and see if your friends do the same. Wear your hair differently. Roll up one pant leg and not the other, then use your influence skills to get others to follow. Come up with something new and observe how others respond.

About Craig Hillier

Craig has been working with teens since 1990 and speaks to over 75,000 young people each year. His high-energy programs and contagious enthusiasm captivate audiences throughout the United States. In addition to leadership keynotes and school assemblies, he focuses his efforts on student leadership training. His one to three-day program is a hands-on approach for today's student leader. Craig was awarded the Outstanding Young Alumni Award from Mankato State University and is a member of the National Speakers Association. He resides in Lakeville, Minnesota with his wife, Kelly and his two children, Derrick and Abigayle.

Winning Edge Seminars
10968 203rd Street West, Lakeville, MN 55044
612-985-5885   fax 612-985-5886   Toll Free: 800-446-3343
Email: winninge@aol.com • Web Site: www.craighillier.com

chapter 4

Building Unity

By Phil Boyte

Creating a Caring CommUnity

LEAD NOW
or Step Aside!

Building Unity

By Phil Boyte

Creating a Caring CommUnity

Butch was sleeping when I walked into his hospital room. I accidentally kicked the chair as I entered and he stirred. His face broke into a smile when I walked in and he said *"Hey, thanks for coming by."* We talked for half an hour or so, first about the car wreck and then about his broken bones. Finally he looked at me and said, *"Phil, I wasn't surprised to see you walk in. We have lunch together almost every day. What has surprised me are the other kids who have stopped by. There are kids that never talk to me at school, but now that I am in the hospital they stop by like they really care. I wonder why they never cared about me this much when I was at school?"*

Isn't it interesting that whenever there is an accident or tragedy at a school, everyone begins to treat each other kindly? Then, after a few months go by, the "casualness" sets in again, and people revert to blatant disregard for one another! I was a senior in high school when Butch had his car accident, but his comment has stayed with me throughout the years. *"I wonder why they never cared about me this much when I was at school?"* Is this true at the school you attend?

Building A Community of Caring People

It is a fact that students who feel connected to their school do not dropout, do not commit acts of violence, and do not create problems at school. Students who feel connected and cared about are comfortable at school and have a sense of belonging. In order to develop unity and belonging on your campus, you need to work from the concept that students who feel connected and cared about want to be at school.

Creating a caring community takes consistent effort by the entire school community. If the students and the adult staff agree to work together, the impact can be significant producing a school where students and teachers feel really good about their community.

Thermometer or Thermostat?

School is simply a small community of people who interact every day. Many students and teachers spend eight to ten hours each day at school and even more hours on the weekend. You and the other students make a choice at your school to be like a *thermometer* or like a *thermostat*. A thermometer indicates the temperature while a thermostat allows you to adjust the temperature and improve the climate. When student leaders act as thermostats, measuring and adjusting the climate of their school, they have the power to improve things and make an amazing difference.

At Monte Vista High in Cupertino, California the student leaders realized the hazing of freshmen was getting out of hand so they decided to make changes to welcome freshmen in a positive, supportive way. They started the Link Crew program to connect successful upperclassmen with incoming freshmen. This transition program assisted freshmen socially and academically from their first orientation to the end of their freshman year. Overall, Monte Vista freshman grades have improved, dropout rates have declined, and the school spirit has risen dramatically. (Contact the author for information about the Link Crew program.)

C.A.R.E.—Four Key Parts to Creating a Caring Community

Communicating Carefully

It's amazing to hear how students talk to each other. Listen in the halls to the comments, the put-downs, and the profanity that students use carelessly between each period. Listen to your friends and even other leaders on campus. It's wild how the negative comments fly between classes and almost stop during the class period, and then start again immediately in the hallways the next hour. What are you saying to each other? Can you really believe your friends respect you when they are constantly commenting on your failures, weaknesses, and struggles? What might happen if you limited your comments to positive words? What would happen if you began to talk a little less and listen a lot more? What if every time you began to say a put-down you stopped yourself and changed that comment to something kind or thoughtful? The high school years are some of the most sensitive days of a person's life and to be constantly teased and joked at can cause a lot of pain.

Keith Hawkins was a student at Garey High School in California who grew tired of the negative climate on his campus. He started lunchtime group he called the

PAC, "Positive Attitude Committee." Anyone could join his group as long as they followed one strict rule; you **had** to be positive. No PAC group member was allowed to put down anyone in, or out of the group. At first, Keith's group was rather small. But he persisted and by the end of his senior year it was the largest group together at lunch! Students bought into the attitude of treating other with respect.

What does your lunch group stand for? What influence can you have on the people you spend time with? The thoughtless comments made in passing so often hurt people at their core.

Think about your clubs, chapters, councils, and friends and what you can do to raise their awareness of how they communicate with other people.

In your next meeting ask people to respond to the following questions:

1. Who is the nicest person at this school? How do they treat you when you walk up?

2. Which person is the hardest to spend time with? What do they do that makes it difficult for others to be around them?

3. What words and phrases are you saying that you need to change? How can you it make it easier for people to be around you?

Accepting Others

Perhaps the greatest challenge you'll face as a leader is interacting with someone who disagrees with you in a passionate way. It doesn't take long to find people who don't agree with you and are not afraid to tell you. What is important is how you react to those people. Granted, it is easier to avoid those who don't agree with you and give them little or no input into the activities and events that happen at your school. These people are often "labeled" and are set aside. This is not good for them, you, or your group.

At Tualatin High in Oregon a campus supervisor told Ms. Biehler, the activities director, about a group of students who were breakdancing behind the school. *"Should we run them off?"* they asked. Ms. Biehler went out and watched for a while and said *"No. Instead, let's invite them to dance for the whole school."* A few weeks later they performed at a pep assembly and received a standing ovation.

What can you do to involve more groups of students and teachers in your activities? How can you involve the "outsiders" and even showcase their talents in front of the entire school? Maybe you could schedule lunch time activities in different parts of the school or host them where different types of students are eating. Display student art in significant places around campus. Put a TV in the hallway and run videos of your fellow students performing their talents. Promote a "battle of the bands" where student bands play. Find "turned-off" students and invite them to get involved in the planning of popular school activities and events to make sure that they are interested and their desires are being represented!

Take a look at your student body at lunchtime. Students eat together in groups of people with whom they share similar interests. Within a few minutes, you will be able to see who the leaders in each group are. Invite some of those leaders to planning meetings and ask for input on activities and ways to bring people together. You all may not be in complete agreement, but you may find a lot of truth in their comments. Before they leave, spend time discussing ways they can get their own friends to be more involved in school activities. Realize when they return to their own groups, they will be watching and waiting to see if any of their ideas are put into action. **Remember: People support what they help create!**

Respect People

After traveling throughout the United States and Canada, I realize that what high school students want most is respect. A student I brought on stage several years ago said to me in a quiet, yet pleading tone, *"Mister, please don't dis me!"* To be disrespected in front of his peers was torture for him. Therefore, I have made it a rule to never disrespect a volunteer from the audience. After years of being treated like a child, teenagers want and deserve respect—and I give it to them!

So why do high school students disrespect each other so often? If it is so important to have respect, why do teens often curse at each other casually and call each other names? Why would they "flip the finger" at each other in both humor and anger? Where does the line of respect start, and where does it stop? If your friends know when you are joking and when you are serious, do those who don't know you understand your intentions?

At a school pep assembly four students were selected from the audience. They were given a caramel apple and told it was a race to see who could eat the apple the fastest. At the whistle they were told to start and keep eating as fast as they could without a break. The whistle blew and away they went. After the third bite two of the students started spitting while the other two just dropped their onion and walked off. The student announcer came forward laughing and explained the caramel apples were really caramel onions! Everyone had a good laugh and the four students went back to their seats.

Following the assembly one of the boys who had eaten the onion approached the rally announcer. He asked, *"Why did you pick me?"* The announcer explained that they'd asked for four volunteers and that he had raised his hand really fast. The boy looked sad and quietly explained, *"I have always been one of the people who sat back and watched you guys do the rallies. I thought they were stupid until last spring when I realized I was missing out on the fun. This summer I decided I wanted to get involved and create some memories. When you guys asked for volunteers I raised my hand fast because I wanted to get involved this year. I always thought you guys respected people more than that."* The boy then dropped his head and walked away.

What if leaders had a rule they would never ask someone else to do something they would not want to have done to them? Would you want to be laughed at by your entire school? Sometimes it seems like something would be funny as long as it happened to someone else. Maybe the easiest way to break down the trust at your school is by disrespecting each other. Trust is essential if you are to build unity at your school.

The skaters at California's Aptos High School were angry because they felt no one respected them. One of them raised the question, *"How can we expect respect if our lunch area looks like a trash tornado hit it every day?"* His friend scoffed, *"No one would even notice if we cleaned it up."* Another friend disagreed, *"Yes, they would."* So, for a week, the skaters made sure their lunch space was spotless. A few days into the experiment people noticed how clean the area was and began asking each other if the skaters were absent. Within a week or two the skaters started noticing how much more respect they were receiving from others.

In order to receive respect, we must be respectable. Here are some guidelines for being respectable.

- Treat others the way you want to be treated.
- Listen politely to the ideas of other people.
- Talk about others in a positive way.
- Allow others to go first.

Most young people deserve the respect of their peers and adults. Keep reminding yourself and your peers to continue to be respectable and the respect will follow. People who feel respected will feel like they belong and want to be part of the school community.

Encourage Others by Your Example

Where do we start to create this caring community? Simple. **Go First!** If you want a friendly school—then

Go First and be friendly. Smile at people. Learn their names and say "hi" in the halls and around town. If you want a clean campus then **Go First** and clean up the lunch area and get your friends to pick up after themselves. If you want a spirited school then **Go First** and be the first to dress up for the spirit day, dance at the dance, and sign-up for the activity! **Go First** by standing and cheering at the pep assembly or at the ball game. **Go First!**

Scott was eating at a burger joint and looked out the window just as the lady threw her napkin and other trash out the car window onto the parking lot. Scott was furious but never said a word as he walked into the parking lot and quietly picked up her trash and tossed it into the can fifteen feet in front of her car. He was careful not to threaten her or even challenge her. He just smiled to himself as he walked back into the restaurant.

We cannot change the world by ourselves, but we can make a large impact if we live what we want to see. The very first thing we need to do when we set this book down is to begin living by what we want to see. So often I complain that other people are not doing what is right. It is here where I need to *go first!* I have to be willing to lead by example and do what I believe in—whether other people are doing that or not! If you want to see the climate at your school get better, then you need to begin to change the way you treat people. You can adjust the thermostat for the better "one act at a time."

Go First! Leaders are always the ones in the front. Talk to your friends, the members of your chapter, club, or council, and meet with your administration and share your ideas. Get them to **Go First** too! When you can mobilize enough people to follow your example, you will begin to see exciting results as others in your community begin to care about each another.

Questions, Activities & Exercises

Have You Noticed?

Have the students in your group pick a partner and look at the person for a few moments. Then, have them turn away from that person and answer the following questions; What color eyes does your partner have? What kind of collar is on your partner's shirt? Have them turn back and see if they answered the questions correctly.

Discussion

How often do we talk with others and fail to notice little things about them like eye color or clothing? What would happen in your organization if people begin to notice the little things about other members? What happens if we pay attention to people's moods and are more patient on the bad days? How would others feel if we noticed when they were not feeling well and did what we could to make their day easier? How would others feel if we were willing to lend them a hand on their busy days?

Make a Point

Label one side of the room A and the other B and tell the students to point to the side they agree with as you read the following statements. As you read each statement, point to the side of the room where your preference lies.

1. If we gave you a drink would you rather have
   A. soda   B. bottled water

2. If we gave you a piece of pizza would you rather have
   A. pepperoni   B. cheese

3. If we gave you a car would you rather drive a
   A. sports car   B. jeep

4. If you had to be one of the following, would you rather be
   A. blind   B. deaf

5. Do you like country music?
   A. yes   B. no

(You can make up your own questions –the more controversial the better—and continue for a few minutes.)

Discussion

Were you surprised at the responses of others in your group?

Does it bother you when other people don't agree with you or share your opinion?

Do you feel it necessary to argue with other people to change their minds to your way of thinking?

Can you accept someone who might feel very different about something that you feel very strongly about?

Go First!

- Write a list of at least three attitudes and behaviors you feel need to be "fixed" at your school in order to improve the overall school climate.

- Write three possible solutions or action steps that you can take to "fix" those things.

- Write down the names of three friends you will get to help you in your mission.

- Write down the date you will put your plan into action.

Remember—*You Go First!*

About Phil Boyte

Phil works with schools who are creating a better place to learn and with young people who want to learn and have fun. Phil is a school climate consultant and a premier youth speaker having addressed youth audiences since 1983. Phil's work has taken him all over the U.S. and Canada and recently to Australia. Phil has developed the internationally recognized Link Crew Orientation Program used to welcome hundreds of thousands of freshmen and new students into high school across the U.S. and Canada. Phil talks to young people of all ages and the adults who support them.

Learning for Living
P.O. Box 279, Meadow Vista, CA 95722
530-878-9520   fax 530-878-9521   Toll Free: 800-874-1100
Email: AskPhil@aol.com • Web Site: www.philboyte.com

chapter 5

Participation and Involvement

By Karl Anthony

How To Get People Tuned Into Your Song!

LEAD NOW
or Step Aside!

Participation and Involvement

By Karl Anthony

How To Get People Tuned Into Your Song!

I overheard a group of adults one day accusing today's teenagers of being "the lazy generation." I kindly interrupted and added, "Did you know the latest research shows that nationally, one-half to two-thirds of middle and high school students participate in community service?" I gazed into their blank, lifeless expressions and then said, "If you think most teenagers spend all their free time hanging at shopping malls, like this one you're hanging in, think again."

Teenagers like you are involved in worthy causes and are making a huge difference in the world. During a recent trip to Nicaragua, I met a group of teenagers who spend much of their free time making friendship bracelets to support their small town where poverty is everywhere you look. This is a country with nearly 60 percent unemployment, yet the leadership of these teens is literally saving their community with the sale of these bracelets. Obviously, these teens know how to stir-up participation and involvement.

My wife, Jeanne and I perform during the summer at a camp for "Kids With Cancer" where 130 kids get to spend one week just being kids instead of the focus being centered around their illness. Each kid has at least one teenage volunteer to help them through the week. By the end of that week, they have become the best of friends. Participation and involvement have great rewards.

How do you get others involved in worthy causes? As a leader, your success depends on your ability to get others interested, involved, and participating in your group's activities and events. You cannot afford to assume that others will get involved just because you are, or because you're enthused, or merely because you ask them to get involved. Effective group participation and involvement takes creative planning and a lot of enthusiasm.

The ideas in this chapter are meant to support your efforts. They will teach you:

How to Get People to Show Up at your Events
How to Get Large Audiences to Participate
How to Get Small Groups to Participate
How to Get Yourself Involved

But first, before you ask *anyone* to do something, realize they will have three important questions in their mind. Any audience, large or small (or for that matter the general public) will ultimately have questions in their mind the moment you try to convince them of something. (Go ahead, put yourself in the position of your audience member.) Say these questions to yourself with a cynical attitude:

Who are you?
Why are you here?
What does this have to do with me?

Start by telling your audience who you are, why you are there, and what your program has to do with them. When your audience has the answers to these questions, they feel at ease and become less cynical and more receptive to participating in an activity, organization, club, or event.

It doesn't matter what you are trying to sell; you could be involved in the most important cause on the planet. To create interest in others, your enthusiasm must show through. You are ultimately selling yourself, offering yourself as the one who has checked out the situation. You're declaring that there is good reason for them to listen to what you are trying to communicate.

Once you are "real" with people and let them know *why* you are so passionate about *what* you believe in, you show them *you* are willing to listen to *them*. Really listen! Then you have set the stage for massive involvement and 100% participation.

How to Get People To Show Up at Your Events

If you want to make certain your activity or event is a smashing success, learn how to tap into the power of *Promotion, Emotion* and *Hoopla!*

Promotion means taking the word of your event and getting it out to the public in a big way. Don't worry about spending a lot of money. If you take a smart approach, you can promote by developing a network of support.

Here are some ideas to get you started:

- Collect email addresses whenever you can. Have those you want on your list fill out a card with their email addresses and then log this list in to your computer. Communicate through this list.

- Create a web page link to offer more information.

- Spread the word through a phone tree. A phone tree starts when you get five people to call five people who call five people who call five people, etc.

- Get free print and radio spots. Good causes deserve good press. Call the media and let them know how important your event is. Then follow up by sending a media release.

Emotion, in this context, refers to the reasons *why* people would want to get involved or participate in your event. In most cases, people will feel the pull to show up when you give them a great reason to show up. Emphasize that reason in your campaign. Your event's posters, flyers, e-mails, media spots, and so on, should all communicate the reason *why* people need to get involved.

Here's an example:

"Don't you believe kids who have cancer deserve at least one week out of the year to just be a kid? Get involved with this summer's 'Kids With Cancer' camp!"

Hoopla is creating "excitement with mystery" or "celebration with intrigue." There are thousands of ways to incorporate Hoopla. Let's use a few examples:

"Come and watch what happens when a 20-pound watermelon is dropped from 60 feet high!" It's good clean fun—that is after someone cleans it up. (A massive watermelon can be displayed in the trophy case for a couple of weeks before the big event to generate the Hoopla!)

"Come honor Mr. Bergren as an outstanding teacher next Wednesday night at a spaghetti social." You can replace your teacher's face on a life-sized cardboard stand-up like Darth Vader, Zena, or Spiderman holding signs such as, "See ya Wednesday night!" As people pass the promotional display, they see the guest of honor. It's goofy but it creates Hoopla!

How to Get Large Audiences to Participate

You have likely been in an audience when the people on stage were extremely boring. Recall what they did to turn off the crowd and don't do the same thing!

Audiences want clear communication and they want to be led by someone with confidence. If the presenter appears unsure, the audience will follow suit. So if you're presenting information to a large group and need to give instructions, be absolutely sure that everyone can hear you and understand what you want them to do.

A simple technique for large group participation is the "Call and Response." Simply say to an audience, *"Repeat after me"* or *"Do what I do."* Start with one line at a time, then have the audience respond. Using this method, if you shouted, "SAY YES!" audience members would be crystal clear what you want them to do and would shout "YES!" Continuing, if you got softer with your command, they would also get softer. If you got louder, they would get louder. They would actually start to mirror your voice and even your body gestures. The wilder you got, the crazier they would get!

Teaching an audience a short phrase or song or perhaps an *energizer* takes a little more preparation. It's important that you know the energizer or song well and are prepared to get the audience involved. Once again, you'd ask for them to follow your words and gestures. It's also helpful to get a few of your friends on stage with you to help teach the activity. If you want to have an audience do energizers and/or songs, start with simple "low risk" activities at first to get them in the mood for playing along. If you ask them to do something really silly right from the start, chances are you'll set a precedent for minimal involvement.

A few other suggestions and tips—

- If you're asking a volunteer or your entire audience to do something outrageous, then you have to be equally outrageous. They will not exceed the energy that you have set.

- When you're teaching hand and body motions, overexaggerate your body movements and be sure everyone can see you.

How to Get Small Groups to Participate

I've found that small groups of 25 or fewer are likely to get involved if you invite them to play a "nonthreatening" game. This is a game where no one loses and no one is made to feel stupid or foolish.

Small group games, when played and processed effectively, will:

- melt the ice and break down the walls that keep people from communicating.

- draw out the quiet people and get them involved and having fun.

- reveal hidden talents. You and the group will find out what skills and talents lie just below the surface of the small group participants.

- change the mood of a group from anxiety to high energy and fun-filled.

- become life solutions. The skills used in games are often the same skills necessary for success in the real world. There are valuable lessons to be learned through games.

Building Trust

After you have set the tone with a game, bring your group together and decide how you can generate a sense of sharing, unity, and trust. Establish some *Group Agreements to* help everyone feel safe and comfortable with each other.

Your list might look like this:

- No put downs.

- Listen when someone else is speaking.

- Positive feedback only.

- Nothing said leaves the group.

- Every opinion is important, etc.

Once your group has created a certain level of trust and teamwork, it is time to move into a deeper level of involvement. Look for activities that directly encourage everyone to keep active in their community, school, or club in the future.

How Do I Get Myself Involved?

Your choice to be a leader is a personal decision. Use that choice to serve and help people. You can be both a leader and a follower in many ways. The decision to strengthen others through leadership will be all the motivation you require to stay involved in an exciting and fulfilling life.

However, remember that being an excellent follower may be the most important leadership skill there is. Never underestimate the power of allowing others to lead. This gives others the chance to be involved and share in the spotlight.

Getting people *tuned into your song* depends greatly on the song you are singing and your level of sincerity. Lift people up as you lead them and show them that getting involved is what life is all about. I hope I get to meet you someday, perhaps working side by side on some worthy cause. Until then, keep singing the song you came to sing!

Questions, Activities & Exercises

Fund-raisers can produce more than funds!

Each fund-raiser you do can build your club's membership. Just make certain that each of the posters, ads, emails, and announcements you use to promote your fund-raiser also clearly communicates who your group is, what your group is about, and how others can get involved.

How would this work?

Suppose you had a car wash and all the volunteers wear the same t-shirt with your club name and logo. Then each customer is given a specially-made flyer or brochure to read while they're waiting. The content in your brochure should be concise and to the point with a brief warm invitation to join or get involved.

Unique Fund-Raising Ideas

Video Game Tournament • Promote a Concert • Stage a Fashion Show • Host a Plant Sale • Sell Pizza By The Slice • Promote a Block Party Yard Sale

The Ultimate in Getting People Involved! Great "A-Thon" Fund Raisers!

- Bike-a-thon (pledges for number of miles/laps ridden)

- Bowl-a-thon (pledges for number of pins knocked down)

- Jog-a-thon (pledges for number of miles/laps jogged)

- Rock-a-thon (pledges for number of hours in rocking chair)

- Skate-a-thon (pledges for number of hours/laps skated)

- Swim-a-thon (pledges for number of laps swam)

- Dance-a-thon (pledges for number of minutes/hours danced)

- Walk-a-thon (pledges for number of miles/laps walked)

Activities for Large Group Participation

Invent a simple but silly handshake. Ask for one volunteer to assist you and show the audience step by step how the handshake goes. Then invite the audience to greet someone they do not know using that handshake.

Don't keep the audience waiting; move along. Acknowledge them when they get it right and tell them to keep using the handshake for the day, a week, the duration of the conference, or even the entire year.

Tell your audience you want to find out how well they will work together as a team. Announce you will count to three (in a foreign language perhaps) and they are to cheer as loud as they can until you count to three again when they are to be instantly silent. A variation is using hand signals instead of counting to three. Always thank them for participating in your research and use this as a transition to begin speaking about teamwork.

Activities or Small Group Participation

Balloon Dragon
Supplies needed: one large balloon per participant

Arrange the group, front to back, in a single file line. Tell the participants to take their balloons, blow them up, and place them between themselves and the person in front of them at stomach or chest level. Each person should then have a balloon pressed against their stomach and back (except for the people at the front and the people at the end of the line.) Tell them *not* to use their hands to keep the balloon in place.

Next, have the whole line move through an obstacle course you have set up to see if they can do it without dropping any balloons. This is a good icebreaker and a great communications exercise. Some variations include the use of blindfolds, or using water balloons if the group is outdoors.

Line 'Em Up!
No supplies needed
Description:

You can make this a competitive game between two groups or a cooperative game against time. Your group is given a task to line up in a specific order, for instance: to line up from the tallest to the shortest, from the youngest to the oldest, alphabetical by first name, by birth date, etc. Be creative with the tasks. You can make the activity more difficult by requiring they complete the task without talking.

About Karl Anthony

His performances are legendary with a sensitivity that involves everyone. Karl has invited hundreds of American youth to the former Soviet Union during the cold war to participate with him in the very first Russian/American Youth Summits in Moscow and gained national attention when asked to perform in the Kremlin. From Red Square to the Great Wall of China, through Central America to the streets of Sydney, Australia, Karl has nurtured youth leadership around the world and he brings those experiences to you. He will move any audience to a level of emotional involvement you never thought possible—a lifetime of inspiration!

Karl Anthony
PO Box 130296, Carlsbad, CA 92013
760-434-5554   fax 760-434-5596   Toll Free: 800-843-0165
Email: karl@karlanthony.com • Web Site: www.karlanthony.com

chapter 6

Team Building

By Michael Scott Karpovich

Breaking the Mold

LEAD NOW
or Step Aside!

Team Building

By Michael Scott Karpovich

Breaking the Mold

True leadership has never really been about a popularity contest or an election, grades or athletic ability, race or faith. Leadership is not about looks or money—leadership is simply a decision. Just like the decision you made to pick up this book and read it, you decide to lead, make a contribution, and leave your legacy!

When I was in school, I was anything but a "leader"! Labeled as "learning disabled" by teachers, "brain damaged" by doctors, "nerd" by peers and "retard" by school bullies, I was, and still am, different than any of the typical leaders in school. I just didn't "fit in"! Looking back, though, perhaps I would have made a great leader, or at least a *different type of leader.*

Unlikely Leaders

Consider how different the environment, activities, and personality of your school, club, or organization would be if your leadership teams were made up of *"unlikely leaders"* instead of just "typical leaders."

What would happen if the class president was an average kid who was really struggling to get a date and good grades? What would the school do if an eleventh grade "tough kid/bully/freak" decided to become president of S.A.D.D. (Students Against Destructive Decisions)? How 'bout if the students voted for a homely nerd to become homecoming queen because she was smart, genuine, kind and consistently went out of her way to help others?

When I was in school, everyone had a place to *hang out* in the halls. There was a corner for religious types, one for jocks, another for each minority, one for band members, a place for geeks, one for freaks, another for hoods, a place for those who fit in and a place for those who didn't. If anyone strayed from his or her "area" too long, it could be uncomfortable.

As a student, I would often look down the hall to where the school leaders stood. There they were—typical leaders: beautiful, successful, popular, athletic, brilliant and some were even elected! Most schools today have a version of that same scene. Why do most school leaders appear the same? There are "unlikely leaders" who would make excellent team players. Effective leaders know how to access this untapped resource, and make these people a part of the team.

The New Team: A Three-Step Approach

Let's set the conventional concept of "team building" on its ear! After we're finished, *leadership* will not be about a small group of people or an individual leading the masses, but a "contagious leadership" that, by its definition, causes everyone to join us as "fellow leaders." Then *together*, we can really make an impact!

First, we have to convince others of the merit of this approach to team building. The objections we will hear are, "I don't want *people like that* on my team!" Some will say, "Oh, *they* will laugh at me or hit me..." Others will suggest that *"these people* are not effective leaders," or *"these people* are part of the problem, *they* can't be part of the solution!"

Our *new* concept of team building flies in the face of bigotry. It is an inclusive team that depends on the diversity of its members.

Truth be known, the naysayers may be right! Some can't stand people who are different, but these bigots will never be real leaders anyway! And if you ask "bullies" to constructively lead, they may think you are just "messing with them." If you nominate a "Geek" to office, he or she may assume that, once again, they are the butt of a joke! Some can't imagine the "burned-out freak" leading a substance abuse prevention group being anything except a joke. (On the other hand, if he/she is genuine, what could be more effective?)

In the end, the strength of our leadership team is its diversity, and its ability to democratically accept all "flavors" of our school's population.

You see, if you refer to any person or group as *"them," "they," "those,"* or *"people like that,"* you are labeling them, and labels are nothing more than "limiters." Whether you are labeled as a leader, jock, freak, band geek, dork, burnout, nerd, religious zealot, dummy, computer nerd, bully, fool, brain, beauty, cheerleader, scholar, or any other descriptor you can think of—all are limiting. No one is simply a "leader" and no individual is simply a "bully"; no one has only one label. In fact, if we look closely, we all have dozens of labels that fit us! Like a diamond, we all have many facets that make us who we are—each facet has its own intrinsic strength.

The Bible teaches us to love our neighbor as we love ourselves—that alone is the most important ingredient of effective team building. To really build your team from the inside out, you need to be quick with compliments and the first to appreciate the uniqueness of your fellow team members.

Remember the advice of the brilliant "philosopher" who told his son Thumper, *"If you can't thay nuffin nice, don't thay nuffin at all."* Disney's *Bambi* is more than a cute children's story. It teaches us that great leaders need to be brave enough to see the good in **everyone**. This is not easy; however, it is essential in the building of a unified team.

Our second step is to find those *yet-to-be-identified "unique leaders."* It would be foolish for us to ask someone to lead simply because he or she has never led before. However, if you see someone with a gift or a willingness to contribute, approach that person. As you help the *unlikely leaders* become great leaders, you make an impact by doing what has never been done before.

Have you ever been chosen last for a team? Do you know anyone who has? If you have ever been left out— congratulations! Strength comes from lessons like these. If not, please know that these people would often do anything to be "included" or valued by their peers (even if they don't act like it). I know for me, it would have made a world of difference if an "A student" smiled at me, or if a popular kid simply said "HI!" Tap into these undiscovered leaders and you tap into your school's undiscovered strength!

Every school or group has its cliques... groups that demand respect, gangs that get no respect and everything in-between! Yeah, there are always some that insist that there are no "cliques"—usually that's because their group is in vogue! If you lead any group, it's necessary to bring together a team of leaders from all perspectives, cliques, groups, and even gangs.

Our third step is to offer new leaders the opportunity to give back. Although it would be cool to change all leadership groups from this point on, do not necessarily immediately appoint these leaders to the highest levels of leadership. Instead, give each individual the opportunity to help out in a small way first. Perhaps you will ask him or her to serve on a committee or do an easy-to-succeed task on the float, pep assembly or student paper. Most of these new leaders have never been asked to contribute—simply asking them can change their lives! **Caution:** If they prove to be effective, don't hesitate to give them bigger responsibilities or opportunities! If you don't, they may interpret it as being ignored or snubbed, and it may cause more damage to your school and its environment.

The Oz Perspective

Rent the movie "The Wizard of Oz," and see it differently than you ever have before. By being observant, you will discover the most amazing story about unique team building.

First there is Dorothy, the traditional leader… nice-looking and basically agreeable. Dorothy may have been an effective leader on Auntie Em's farm, but it wasn't until a tornado tore her house from its foundations and smashed it to the ground far from Kansas, that she discovered her true leadership ability!

The Munchkins worshiped Dorothy for landing her house on the "bad witch." A typical leader may say, "Hey, I like to be worshiped… I'm staying here!" But not Leader Dorothy! She decided to head off into the unknown. Why? Not because she was strong, independent and easily confused for a "good witch"… she decided to head down the Yellow Brick Road because of what she didn't have. (She didn't have her Kansas home.) She led not because of what she did have; she led because of what she lacked.

So Dorothy boogies down the road, followed by the ever-happy, ever-yipping Toto (everyone should have perpetually happy followers like Toto). Then she comes upon the Scarecrow (my personal favorite—"brain damaged" like me) who joins her as a "peer-leader." Why is the Scarecrow so cool? Not because he is filled with straw, but because he has no brain! Think about it. If he had a brain, would he and his straw-filled body have attacked the fire-throwing witch? His greatest moments could not have happened if he had a brain! His strength is because of his lack.

Movin' on down the road, our two mutual leaders (and Toto) come upon the third teammate—The Tin Man. Again, what makes the Tin Man join "Dot" & "the Crow"? Not because he had an axe and an impenetrable suit of armor. He led because of what he *didn't* have. He was heartless! And because he didn't have a heart, he was able to make the tough decisions.

Do you see how teamwork builds on each other's weaknesses as well as each other's strengths? It's not simply about what you have; it's also what you *don't* have!

As the three of them (and Toto) continue, they come upon our fourth "peer leader"—the Cowardly Lion! The Lion joins the leadership team not because of his strong roar and frightful appearance but because he is a coward. You may ask what value is cowardice in leadership? Well, what one person may call cowardice, another would call caution. No one individual led the others—arm-in-arm all of them together went "off to see the wizard"! Can you see how the team's strength and drive came from the adversity that each unique member experienced?

Why is "The Wizard of Oz" still so popular after all these years? Because all the leaders are so very different. There is someone and something for everyone. That difference is what makes them winners; it is what makes them fun; it is what makes them so enjoyable to watch. It is what leads to their success.

Imagine, for a second, what a weak story it would be if there were four Dorothys or four Cowardly Lions. Too many leadership teams are made up of the same type of people! In fact, imagine the story if only *one* of these very different leaders was missing. What would it be without a Scarecrow or Tin Man? The team's strength lies in its variety, in its diversity!

Translate this to *your* team. Your team will be strong because of its variety. You must have the courage to find people who are completely different from yourself. Don't reject the weaknesses of others but consider how those weaknesses can become assets to your leadership team. Some individuals do "get into trouble," but that rebel aspect could be channeled into a powerful leadership trait!

The Commencement

Years ago, I had the opportunity to speak at a kindergarten graduation. Picture this scene: I stood on stage in the middle of a gymnasium, the parents sat in the bleachers while 15 graduating kindergartners sat in their tiny chairs, proudly wearing construction paper graduation caps with yarn tassels. They were as solemn as any five or six-year-old could be. One little boy looked up at me, and with hands firmly placed on his hips, said, "I'm only six years old and I'm graduating! My brother waited until he was eighteen!" This was obviously the most important day in their lives!

I invited all the graduates to join me on stage to play "follow-the-leader." (What a great tool to demonstrate leadership!) I told the boy at one end of the line that he was the leader. He crossed his arms and gleefully said, "COOL!" I then asked everyone to turn in the other direction. I told the girl at the other end of the line that *she* was now the leader. She said in a matter-of-fact tone, "I knew that!" Next, I had the kids face their parents and told them they were now *all* leaders! One girl said, "But nobody is following!" (Too often, true leadership is just like that. We lead and no one follows.) Finally, I told the leaders to face the opposite direction and said, "Now you're all leaders and look who's following!" One boy said joyfully, "Now Mom, you follow me!"

Yes, I know that "follow-the-leader" is a child's game, but I came to several profound conclusions from this simple exercise.

First, we are most effective if we all lead together!

Second, sometimes you become the leader simply because you're in the front. Many leaders are not leaders by choice or merit; most are leaders by default—and nothing could cause more damage to a worthwhile goal!

Third, sometimes kindergartners do lead their parents, students lead their teachers, employees lead their employers, the meek and mild lead the powerful and strong. Some suggest that leadership comes from above rather than below, or that you must be very accomplished before you can do anything worthwhile. The truth is some of the greatest ideas or plans come from the least likely places.

Whether you are a *"typical leader"* or a potential *"unique leader,"* realize that you can be part of a team, lead the team and even inspire others to lead with you. Some of the world's greatest leaders have been men and women who have led in a very lonely way—and made their greatest impact with little or no support. However, if we all lead *together* towards a common goal, we will make the *greatest* impact and it will become irrelevant if anyone follows as long as we do not lead alone!

Questions, Activities & Exercises

- With your current leadership team or a friend, discuss who would make a powerful "unique leader" in your school.

- Brainstorm five ways you can find and approach potential "unique leaders" and get them involved without insulting or offending them.

- Develop a comprehensive list of basic tasks that new leaders can try as they take on more and more responsibilities. Remember, many of these people have never been asked to help... just asking may change their lives.

Six **TEAM BUILDING** Keys to Remember and Practice:

1. Challenge yourself to find at least one leadership partner. Too often people try to make an impact alone. Although these lonely leaders have at times made a significant impact, many have given up in despair! You can't approach leadership or team development alone.

2. Get together with your partner, or better yet—your entire team. Pop tons of popcorn and rent a video like "Bambi" or "The Wizard of Oz." As you watch, look for a new perspective on the total team concept and leadership development. (Other great "team" movies that profile unlikely leaders include "Revenge of the Nerds," "Dead Poets Society," "Lucas," and "Jack.") Discuss your opinions and insights about team building after viewing the movie.

3. Have enough courage to look into *everyone's* eyes (not just your teammates') and greet them with a smile. No one has more power to impact the esteem of a student than another student! It is casual contacts like these that can lead to optimum team building.

4. Together with your partner or team, seek out "unlikely leaders" who are different from you. Approach these individuals and encourage their involvement by asking them to take an active role in an activity.

5. Support the ideas of the "unlikely leaders." Sometimes an activity or "cause" may not get everyone jazzed, but the more "unique leaders" you have on the team, the more diverse and dynamic the activities!

6. Evaluate what has happened and then start the process all over again!

About Michael Scott Karpovich

Diagnosed with *brain damage* at age four, beaten up and called a "NERD" by peers... this unlikely hero has discovered that our greatest adversities are really what make us strong! This advocate of Nerds has worked successfully as a farmer, a popular disc jockey, a high school drama coach, a counselor, a college instructor and now as a Certified Speaking Professional! Described as half Robin Williams and half Wayne Dyer, Michael speaks to over 300,000 people annually. (*Not bad for a brain-damaged nerd!*)

Michael Scott Karpovich, CSP
220 North Almer, Box 272, Caro, MI 48723-0272
517-673-3036   fax 517-673-0116   Toll Free: 800-718-3367
Email: Michael@Karpovich.com • Web Site: www.karpovich.com

chapter 7

Follow Through

By Eric Chester

Don't "tion" (shun) Away the Important Stuff!

LEAD NOW
or Step Aside!

Follow Through

By Eric Chester

Don't "tion" (shun) Away the Important Stuff!

All in favor, say "Aye."
All opposed, say "Nay."

The "ayes" have it. We will do a ____
(bake sale, car wash, carnival, dance, pizza party, etc.)

If you're reading this book, you've obviously been through this portion of a meeting numerous times. Someone in your group (club, chapter, council, etc.) brings up an idea for an activity or event. It starts with some exciting brainstorming followed by a discussion and a vote. If the motion passes, you are now at the crossroads—it's time to take what was once only an idea and turn it into a smashingly successful activity or event.

But how?

First, realize what you are up against. Everyone in the meeting is excited and wants to be a part of great new activity. So when it's time to vote for another member's idea, it's only natural (and polite) to say, *"yeah . . . let's do it!"* But when it's time to do the actual work, many who voted the idea "in" can't be found. Sound familiar?

One way to reduce the "I vote *yes* to the idea but *no* to my being involved" syndrome is to build accountability into your voting procedure. Rather than asking for "ayes" and "nays," ask for a show of hands from those people who *commit* their personal involvement. Using a club roster, have the group secretary record the names of those who raise their hand. Post the list of "committed" people for this activity in front of the meeting room. Keep it posted for all to see until the event is over or the activity complete. That's when you compare the list of people who pledged their involvement with a list of those who actually got involved.

Share this information with the entire group. When your members realize they are committing themselves to actually *participate* when they vote, they will be more inclined to speak up for only those activities and projects they really support. This way, you get an accurate read on the real interest in any particular activity.

Assuming you now have a list of *committed* people ready to do a great *activity*, how can you as a leader ensure its success?

Two Words with One Gigantic Outcome

That's what this chapter is all about. Follow Through — two small words with one gigantic outcome. Follow Through is the difference between an activity that bombs, and one that is 'da bomb!

Four critical "tions" make Follow Through happen: Delega*tion*, Communica*tion*, Promo*tion*, & Apprecia*tion*.

Delegation

Delegation is a fancy word that essentially means deciding "who does what." If you've ever been to a barbeque when there were a zillion burgers but *no* buns, you've experienced poor delegation. Obviously everyone was told to bring "something"; they just weren't told "what."

The first key to Follow Through is knowing how to delegate. That does not mean you need to know how to boss others around. Instead, leaders need to make certain all the details are being looked after, and that those who agree to take on a specific responsibility live up to their commitment.

If you are the leader or "chair" of an activity, follow these simple delegation guidelines (and if you are indirectly responsible for overseeing the activity, make certain those in charge follow these steps):

1. Before you get started, draw up a plan. Make a complete list of what the activity will require in the way of money, facilities, promotional materials, chaperones, volunteer help, donations, equipment, prizes, clean up, etc.

2. Gather an activity committee. Get committee members to sign up for the duties and specific details of your plan. Make certain they know what they are agreeing to do, and have them sign their names on your list right beside that responsibility. *TIP: Don't spread anyone, including yourself, too thin. Make certain to distribute the workload evenly. If you

can't get enough people to help, reconsider whether the activity should be attempted at all!

3. For the really big details, always assign a back-up person. For example, if you are planning a huge marathon volleyball game in a remote location to raise money for charity, make certain you ask more than one person to be responsible for bringing the key ingredients like balls and nets!

4. After you do the first three steps thoroughly, stand back and let your volunteers do what they have agreed to do. The quickest way to de-motivate people is to do their job for them!

The danger of delegating lies in getting carried away and having others see you as a dictator. Some leaders get "power hungry" and abuse their position. If you step back and see yourself ordering people around, you could be heading for a breakdown. Sure, they may follow your directions for awhile, but soon they will rebel. So make certain you ask nicely, clarify the desired outcome, and offer to assist them any way you can.

Communication

In school, you've probably had a class or two in which students played the "rumor game." In this game, one person is given a written sentence to memorize and then sent out of the room to repeat that sentence to another person. Then another volunteer goes out into the hall where they the second person repeats the message. This third person tells a fourth person who tells a fifth person, and so on until the last person who receives the message comes back in the room to repeat the sentence in front of the entire room. When the first person reads the original sentence, everyone erupts into laughter. They immediately see how "butchered" the message has become.

It's not quite as funny when several people show up at the school on Saturday morning for the car wash, only to find out they were supposed to meet at the park. Or when a few of your members suddenly come to the conclusion (after waiting an hour in a downpour) that the softball picnic was not this Sunday but next Sunday. Nothing can destroy a group's spirit faster than a communication breakdown.

As a leader, it is vitally important to keep your people informed. Although it is difficult to completely eliminate communication problems, the following reminders can help you keep everyone on the same page:

- Inform your entire group of a central place they can go for up-to-date club news and information. This way, if they miss a meeting, they can still get the specifics by referring to a bulletin board or website.

- Make a list of important names and numbers, including all the members and advisors of your club or group. Keep that list with you. Consider the advantages of distributing a member directory.

- When you need people to gather, be sure to give them clear, concise details. Include an agenda, maps, directions, phone numbers, and any other pertinent information. Also, show dates, times, and what you want those attending to bring—e.g., money, special clothing, equipment, etc.

- Before you distribute any written information, pretest its effectiveness by showing it to several "outsiders" and asking them to interpret it for you. (This is similar to the last step in the rumors game.)

Remember, any precautionary efforts you take to protect the flow of valid, up-to-date information between club members, officers, and advisors will pay off in the long run. You'll have bigger turnouts and smaller headaches.

Promo*tion*

The key to a successful activity is involvement. And the key to getting people involved is promotion. After all, you cannot attract people to an activity they do not know about any more than you can have them return from a place they have never been.

Promotion is perhaps the most important—yet most overlooked—phase of student activities. Product marketers spend huge sums of money to get consumers to recognize their brand names and buy their goods and services. You can learn from them! Apply a few successful marketing principles to generate enthusiasm and involvement in your promotional campaign.

To get "tapped" into the minds of the people you want to attract, apply this TAP formula for promotion:

T - Theme your promotional materials by tying all aspects of the promotion directly to the event. The colors, illustrations, lettering, text, and design of the promotional materials should look the same so that people can visually associate each ad or poster with that specific event. Your announcements or radio ads should all use the same music, words, announcer, etc. (If you see a swoosh logo, you know it's from Nike; if you hear "you've got mail" you know it's an ad for AOL.)

A -Always give specifics. Don't make the public strain to see or hear the details, specifically the "what, when, where, how much, etc." Make absolutely certain each promotional piece you mail, post, or broadcast provides complete details about the activity. It must also alert readers and listeners where to go for more information.

P - Position your materials to bombard the segment of the population you want to attract. If you want your event to be attended by young kids, place your materials in places where young kids will see them, e.g., grade schools, playgrounds, etc. If your event is for parents, put your promotional budget into sending a home-mailer or purchasing an ad on a local radio station that's popular with parents. If it's for students at your school, use every medium available to you to get the word out, e.g., morning announcements, school paper, flyers on cars in the parking lot, posters in halls, etc. *TIP: Always get the necessary authorization, permission, and/or approval before you post materials. *You wouldn't want someone to walk into your room and just start putting up posters without your permission, would you?*

Last but definitely not-to-be-forgotten—develop an easy-to-duplicate set of mailing labels for all the major local media sources in your area. Each time your group promotes an activity, put together a letter or postcard "news release" with all the pertinent details, then send it out to all the newspapers and radio/TV stations on this list. You will be amazed at how many times your event or activity shows up on the 6 o'clock news or makes the headlines!

Appreciation

Think back to the last time you petted a dog. Got the picture in your mind? Good. Then ask yourself these questions...

Why did you pet that dog? What did *you* get out of it?

The dog couldn't do your homework for you. He couldn't clean your room or baby-sit your kid sister for you. Dumb thing couldn't even pet you back!

So once again, why did you pet the dog? The answer? He returned sincere appreciation. It was that adorable look on his little face that said, "Thank you...this feels *soooo* good!"

Like dogs, people thrive on appreciation. It is perhaps the greatest motivator in the world, and a "must" for every student leader's toolbox. To be an effective leader, focus on perfecting the art of saying "thanks."

Some of the best student groups I've ever worked with claim their success results from their focus on giving recognition and appreciation. Many of these clubs, teams, and chapters have a specific officer whose sole job is to send "thank you" notes and find creative ways to recognize their participants.

Whom should you thank? Only those who go out of their way to help you, the ones who do special things for you and the group. For starters, how about your parents, teachers, coaches, and your advisor(s)? And don't forget administrators, chaperones, sponsors, cooks, and janitors. If a business donated to your cause, thank 'em. If you received publicity on the radio or in the papers, thank the person responsible. It's far better to say thanks to someone who might not deserve it than to risk not thanking someone who *does* deserve it. So be generous, but sincere.

Also, thank the members of your club or team. Recognize their participation and reward their excellence. If a reporter interviews you for an article in the paper, share the credit with your teammates. Give the names of those who helped and especially those who exceeded the standard. In your meetings, announce the names of "star contributors" to the other members and lead them in a round of applause.

How should you say thanks? That really depends on what you're saying thanks for. With little things—like when a custodian comes to unlock a door for you—a simple verbal "thank you" will suffice. But also realize that TALK IS CHEAP! If an adult—any adult—gives time and energy to support your club with an activity, **go out of your way** to show what it means to you! Cards, plaques, t-shirts, and small-personalized gifts are great ways of saying "we couldn't have done this without you!"

When should you say thanks? Immediately. There is no better time than the present to share feelings of appreciation with another person. If you don't say thanks soon enough, you risk being viewed as unappreciative. You can also keep a record of those who support you the most and throw an appreciation event like a breakfast or banquet in their honor. Do this at the end of your year as a terrific way to show your appreciation for those special parents, advisors, coaches, administrators, and community leaders who supported your organization.

Your Success Depends on Follow Through

The Follow Through of leadership is like the transmission of a sports car; it's not the *flashy* part, but the darn thing won't run without it. Simply put, your effectiveness as a student leader is in direct proportion to your degree of "follow through" with the gritty details.

Don't shun the four "**tions**" of Follow Through! Delega**tion,** Communica**tion,** Promo**tion,** and Apprecia**tion.** *In fact, give them your special atten**tion!***

If you apply some of this chapter's simple ideas and take the prescribed action, your whole leadership experience will be much more fun, rewarding, and trouble free!

Questions, Activities & Exercises

You are the chairman of the decoration committee for the prom. All those who attend know that **you** are responsible for the prom's atmosphere. Wanting to make it the best ever, you realize you need a lot of help getting supplies and materials. You also know you will need a lot of help with the actual decorating. Unfortunately, only two other people have volunteered to help you.

1. How can you find more help and be absolutely positive that those who verbally commit will actually show and help?

2. How will you determine which people will do which things? What is the best way for assigning tasks to specific people?

3. You show up to the hotel where you're having the prom and they inform you that, because of a broken water pipe, you cannot have access to the room for decorating until three hours before the prom starts. You thought you'd have all day (a Saturday) and your 15-person decorating committee is scheduled to come within the next hour. What will you do?

Your club has voted to do a community dog wash (like a car wash except owners pay your group to wash their pets instead of their cars) to raise money to send *you* to a national leadership conference. They have elected you to be activity chairperson. The club members are enthusiastic and really want to help you! You are allergic to dogs, but you're determined to make the event a wild success anyway.

1. How would you set out to plan this activity?

2. What do you see as the major tasks to be addressed in making this event successful?

3. List at least five different low-or-no cost strategies for notifying your *entire* targeted community about this unusual activity?

4. Considering your allergy, what are several ways you can still be present and involved?

5. Mr. Jigbottom at PetsRUs donates three boxes of soap. An assistant principal, Ms. Shakerbee, gives up her whole Saturday to supervise (school rule) and Jenny Jenkins' mom, a vet, stays the whole day to help. Also, 18 members and your club's advisor show up to wash dogs. What are some unique things you could do to show your gratitude?

About Eric Chester

For more than a decade, Eric has been preparing teenagers for the real world, and preparing the world for a new generation. His acclaimed presentations have empowered 1.5 million students, parents, educators, and business professionals worldwide. Eric is synonymous with leadership, keynoting as many as 50 large student leadership conferences each year, including the National Association of Student Councils, Key Clubs, DECA, FBLA, FFA, SADD, 4H, etc. He is the founder, co-author, and publisher of the best-selling Teen Power series, and his sixth book "Employing Generation Why" will be released in early 2,000. He lives with his wife and four teens in Lakewood, Colorado.

Generation Why, Inc.

1410 Vance Street – Ste. #201, Lakewood, CO 80215
303-239-9999   fax 303-239-9901   Toll Free: 800-304-ERIC
Email: eric@ericchester.com • Web Site: www.generationwhy.com

Part Two

Internal Wiring

chapter 8

Faith

By Byron V. Garrett

"Dream Makers...
Dream Busters"

Faith

By Byron V. Garrett

"Dream Makers...Dream Busters"

*"In the absence of true leadership, people will listen
to any voice. Even when it's the wrong voice.
In fact, people have such faith, they'll walk
through the desert to a mirage looking for water
and drink the sand. They don't drink the sand
because they are thirsty; they drink the sand
because they don't know the difference."*
– The Film, *American President*

Without question or doubt, you are on the road to identifying, tapping, and maximizing your leadership potential. There is a true leader in everyone...some must search deep down on the inside, but the leader is there. Watching and waiting, believing and hoping the day will come when the true leader will rise from the depth of your soul.

I've discovered throughout my years that many people develop a strong sense of determination. Most leaders in the making fine-tune the real skills needed for success. (i.e., teamwork, effective communication, the art of delegation). However, many forget one of the most critical ingredients to leadership success...FAITH...a simple but powerful word that separates the important from the less important, the dream makers from the dream busters.

FAITH, in its most basic form, is a high level of belief. Belief in what, you may ask? Belief in one's self. All too often, people spend their lives, their time, and their talents striving for great successes only to be met with disappointments and heartaches. *There is power in believing.* I'm not saying your world will change tomorrow because of your level of belief. The impossible may not be possible overnight; however, it can become possible over time.

Positive Thinking

As you venture through this game called life, you will discover that most successful people have mastered the power of positive thinking. My grandmother always said, *"Don't expect what you don't expect."* Maybe you decide you want to become Vice President of an organization. You begin campaigning and convincing others why you would be an awesome VP. However, when you get home in the afternoon and you're all alone, there is no one in your corner but you. A voice from nowhere says, *"You are not ready, you are not capable, and you are not prepared."* Something begins to question who you are, where you are going, and how you will get there. Many refer to this questioning as self-doubt. Unfortunately, most battles are not lost on the battlefield, but are lost through self-doubt and disbelief. People are defeated time and time again...not by arch rivals but by themselves. Know this: *When you truly believe, success is not a matter of if, but a matter of when.*

You are poised, positioned, and prepared for success. But one question remains unanswered, *"If not now, then when…if not you, then who?"* What or whom are you waiting on to turn your stumbling blocks into stepping stones or your obstacles into opportunities? There may be thousands who would just as well have you give in, give up, and give out.

The only opinion that directly impacts your success or failure is *your* opinion. I hate to be the bearer of bad news, but until you believe that you deserve better or that you can do better, your life will not change. I believe in you. Also your parents, friends, and many others believe in your potential. However, until you grasp hold of your future and stay true to your dreams, you will remain a dream buster, not a dream maker.

Somewhere along the way, people like you and I begin listening to voices other than our own. Voices that would have us believe, *"You couldn't, you shouldn't, you never will, you just won't."* You give in to this *stinking thinking*. That's right, STINKING THINKING! It stinks of negativity, foul thoughts, and no faith.

Know That You Know

When you desire something, you must be realistic and honest. You must know that you know that you know. For example, in high school I wanted very badly to be the quarterback or wide receiver on our football team. However, I had to be honest with myself to know that I lacked the physical ability (speed, agility, etc.) to make the cut. I assessed the situation and decided I would not place myself in a position that could result in failure. The truth of the matter was this: I didn't believe I was up to the task. I hadn't practiced nor played as often as the other individuals trying out for the team. I knew deep down I did not have what it would take. But I really did believe that my purpose at school was big…bigger than I would have ever imagined. Yet my purpose was not to become the football star because I had not prepared.

Understand this: I'm not saying don't try different things. I am saying that you have to determine what gifts, talents, and skills compose you…those things that come easy to you but difficult to others. I realized that, though I lacked the skills to be a great football player, I possessed strong communication, organization, and networking skills. Instead of becoming the football star, I became Secretary for the Student Body Cabinet…a position I hadn't given much thought to, but began to work toward when I recognized my true potential. I had gone beyond believing for I knew in my heart this was my place; it was my moment to make my mark.

Begin to Believe

Many will enter your life and strive to persuade and dissuade you. No one, including your parents, knows *you* better than you know yourself. Why do I say this? Because you have the ability to dazzle and amaze everyone including yourself…like the time when you weren't pulling your weight in class and your parents really believed the best grade you could get was a C. Of course, they only believed it because you convinced them you were giving your all. Then, as the semester came to a close and you received your report card, everyone was surprised to see that your C had risen to an A. In that case, something on the inside clicked and you began to focus—you began to believe.

You were determined to do better for one simple reason...because you knew and believed you were better than average. However, had you thought as your parents, teachers, or even your friends did, you would still have a C instead of the A that you earned. The funny thing about a C...it represents average. *It is your right not to be average.* Average is merely top of the bottom, bottom of the top—somewhere stuck in the middle. People remember great successes and great failures, but not the average.

Do you know the difference between average and outstanding, the difference between mediocrity (status quo) and excellence? *FAITH.* Along the way, average people only focus on meeting the basic needs. They never focus on exceeding expectations. They lack the will power and belief system that can transform the ordinary into the extraordinary. When no one else believes, you've got to...it's critical that, even in the worst of times, you can believe. Your family may turn their backs on you and your friends may become quite few but you've got to believe...you've got to have faith.

Work Toward Your Goals

Faith power works wonders. A wise person once said that, *"Faith, without works is dead."* Simply put, it's great to believe—but if you are not constantly working toward your goals, toward your objectives, they won't happen. *You have to work to make things happen.* No matter how much faith you possess, unless you put something in, you will get nothing out. It's like being thirsty and having an empty cup...no matter how much you desire to no longer be thirsty, the situation will not change until you take action. When you decide to move from belief to action by placing water or another liquid in the cup, then and only then will your faith work wonders.

Living Their Faith

I can recall a gentleman named Elias Howe. Elias was a poor man who believed that someone could invent a contraption or machine that would place clothes together instead of having them sewn by hand. As Elias traveled the world trying to convince others to help fund his project, people literally laughed at the mere thought of doing things differently. As time passed, Elias spent all he had to create something called a sewing machine. To this date, the sewing machine has become an everyday item creating billion-dollar empires...all because Elias believed a machine could make the clothes he never had money to buy and he lived that belief.

Have you encountered those people who try to rain on your parade...those people who convince others you've just lost it and gone crazy? What do you do when others walk out because they can't catch your vision? That moment—when it seems all hope is gone—you must believe there's no way you can fail. I say this because Walt Disney faced such situations. Remember, he's the looney one who told the world we would be entertained by a black and white mouse by the name of Mickey. You know the man, whom everyone thought was crazy when he started building an entertainment complex around the swamplands of Florida. You know the park as Disney World. Yes, people not only thought Walt was crazy, they had the nerve and audacity to tell him so. But of course, he persevered and created a multibillion-dollar empire that has created products and parks from Japan to California and Europe to Florida. What's so different about Walt and you? *Your level of faith.* It can reach beyond this atmosphere.

"C" Your Way to Success

As you journey through life—the leaders of tomorrow will be those of you who *"C" YOUR WAY TO SUCCESS!*

*Change Your Mindset...*leadership success awaits you.

No question about it. To make it to the top, you must change your mindset, creating a positive talk, a positive walk, and a positive life. Your level of belief must be strong enough to rise as others turn their backs. A change in mindset will cause you to continually evaluate yourself, assessing where you are and where you want to be. Others won't understand. In fact, they won't have a clue. They fail to recognize the greatness within themselves, let alone you. Many will question and many may doubt, but you must stay focused and determined.

As you read this book, you could have a change in mindset. You cannot embrace this information and stay as you are. It's not that the world will change around you, but rather your eyes will not see things the same way they have in the past. Your mind will process information differently than before. A change in mindset will free you to explore, take calculated risks, and reach beyond your comfort zone.

Challenge Yourself. All the great leaders—present and past—exceed expectations.

Now that you know faith power works wonders, you have to be willing to do today what others won't—to have tomorrow what others never will. That means part of challenging yourself means sacrifice. You would not be hearing the whole truth if I left that out!

Challenging yourself or pushing the boundaries to reach the stars requires you to do things differently than before. You cannot get tomorrow's success with yesterday's work. *Are you willing to live the next 2-3 years like most won't so that you can live the next 20-30 years like many never will?* When life gets rough at the end of the rope, you must either find the strength to endure or swing to another rope because you have options.

I recall an African proverb that says: *Every morning in the jungle a gazelle and lion awake. The gazelle knows that as the sun comes up, it must outrun the fastest lion in order to survive. The lion knows that as the sun rises it must outrun the slowest gazelle in order to survive. No matter whether you're a lion or gazelle, one thing is certain; when the sun comes up you best be running.* CHALLENGE YOURSELF.

Courage To Commit… and hear the wake-up call around the globe today.

It's a call for the competent, courageous, and prepared—those who refuse to settle for less which is not more and those who ignore another's perception of who you are, where you are going, and how you will get there.

The call is for you. The future teachers and preachers, businessmen and women, designers and manufacturers because you have the courage. Because you possess faith, you will explore and develop, research and write, own and operate. In fact, you are transforming from a leader of tomorrow to a leader of today. It takes a strong person to adhere to Ralph Waldo Emerson's charge of not going where the path may lead, but going where there is no path and leaving a trail.

Douglas Mallock said, *"If you can't be a pine on top of the hill, be a shrub in the valley, but be the best little shrub by the side of the hill; if you can't be a bush, be a tree; if you can't be a highway, just be a trail; if you can't be the sun, be a star—for it isn't by size that you win or fall, just be the best of whatever you are!"*

If you apply the 3 Cs to every facet of your leadership experience, you will excel and achieve your dreams. Life is tough and you may get knocked down a couple of times, but know you are not knocked out. You will make a comeback. Every day you rise is a new day…a new opportunity to make history. You have 24 hours day, 7 days a week, 365 days a year. How you use or loose them is completely up to you. Go and be a dream maker today!

FAITH COMMITMENT CREED

Beyond Impossibilities Are
Powerful Possibilities;
Beyond Obstacles Are
Obvious Opportunities;

Beyond Stumbling Blocks Are
Superb Stepping Stones;
Beyond Thunderstorms Are
Triumphant Rainbows.

I Am Unable To Do It All...
But Will Do That Which I Can.
What I Could Do, I Should Do,
What I Should Do, I Shall Do!
I Am Successful

Questions, Activities & Exercises

Answer yes or no to the following questions:

_____Do I complete what I begin?

_____Do I practice my goals in preparation for success?

_____Do I allow people to get me off track?

_____Do I give in to others thoughts about me?

_____Do I continually visualize my success?

_____Do I talk about my plans in a positive way?

_____Do I know where I'm going in my life?

Provide your own answers to the following:

1) My goal is _____ (be specific regarding something you want to accomplish in the next 3-6 months).

2) In order to make this a reality, I must do these…(list specific actions):

_____   _____

_____   _____

_____   _____

3) I believe this will come to pass because _____

_____ !

4) I deserve this because _____ !

In working with business executives, student leaders, and entertainers, I have found the following principles work best in "keeping the faith":

1. Always use words such as *I, my, mine,* and *me.* They will personalize your statements and make them more believable.

2. Keep your positive thoughts in the present tense. Speaking in terms of the past discounts the affirmation of your goals.

3. Make your goals short and easy to remember (brief phrases).

4. Think/speak in positive terms so your mind doesn't replay negatives. You want to focus on the outcome, not the issue.

5. Write down your goals using positive language.

6. When people speak negatively, turn their words into a positive.

Top 10 Reasons
For Being A Dream Maker,
Not A Dream Buster

10. If not now, then when? If not you, then who?

9. Avoid average—top of the bottom, bottom of the top!

8. You only live once.

7. Gotta love yourself!

6. Find something in life you love doing, that you'd do it for free, but do it so well you get paid for it!

5. Nothing ventured nothing gained.

4. Get to a point that you do things because you want to, not because you have to!

3. You did then as you knew then,
   You know better so you do better,
   When you do better, you live better.

2. Take a pause for the cause

1. You Deserve It!

About Byron V. Garrett

Known as SPKR4LIFE, Byron serves as President of Life Works International. From Nigeria to the Bahamas, New Jersey to the Cayman Islands, Byron travels the globe—preparing tomorrow's leaders, today...through motivational presentations and leadership training. Garrett often serves as a featured speaker for youth organizations like HOSA, FBLA, Rotary International, and Pride World Drug Conference. Host of the international television & radio program Life Break, Byron writes a weekly syndicated column—Keepin It Real. Author of 4 books—The ABC's of Life, being the most notable, Byron strives to challenge thoughts, change minds, and offer the courage to commit.

Life Works International
1385 N. 44th Street, Phoenix, Arizona 85008
602-286-9633   fax 602-462-5530
Email: spkr4life@lifeworks101.com • Web Site: www.lifeworks101.com

chapter 9

Character

By Bobby Petrocelli

It's the LITTLE Things that Make a BIG Difference

LEAD NOW
or Step Aside!

Character

By Bobby Petrocelli

It's the LITTLE Things that Make a BIG Difference

Think of the Olympic athletes who dedicate thousands of hours of hard work and sacrifice to reach their goals. An Olympic gymnast, for example, spends 20,000 hours preparing for one big moment of competition.

Life works the same way—all the LITTLE efforts combined prepare you to face anything that life throws your way. Taking the easy path usually leads to destruction, while the disciplined and responsible path leads to fulfillment.

Being faithful in the LITTLE things also prepares you to be faithful when it comes to bigger things. If you forgive the minor trespasses, you will forgive the major ones, too. If you love the least, you will be able to love the greatest. If you give when you have little, you will give when you have much.

The following eight points and examples bring out details to help you see how the LITTLE things develop character—he kind of strong character you want.

1. Putting others before yourself is the true measure of character.

Words such as honor, integrity, patience, loyalty, honesty, kindness, and compassion are all qualities of character. But "character" could best be described as *SERVANTHOOD!* This is when people are willing to lay down their lives for a friend. It is putting the needs and desires of another above your own.

Loving unselfishly doesn't mean making the *least* of yourself, but making the *most* of others. This thought can transform your relationships. One of the greatest examples of true character during the 20th Century was Mother Theresa. She gave and asked for nothing in return.

To know if you are giving enough, compare your employment income records with your records of gift-giving to accurately measure your degree of commitment.

True character is also measured by the number of lives you touch, not by the amount of material possessions you obtain. Always remember to put others before yourself.

2. Everyone who lightens the burden of others is useful in this world.

The message conveyed in the movie "Patch Adams" is phenomenal. The doctor Patch Adams (played by Robin Williams) performed his medical duties differently than other doctors. His goal: treat the patient as well as the disease, and whether the patient lives or dies, everyone still wins. Patch wanted everyone to be treated with dignity. He believed that each person had a name, not just a label—patient #32 with a certain disease. Throughout the movie, he adjusted to every situation so he could be all he could be to serve hurting people. He didn't just have sympathy; he had compassion. This movie is based on the true life story of Patch Adams.

I define compassion as hating *a person's problem so much that you are compelled to do everything in your power to help get rid of it.* Patch would enter a ward with sick children, dress up like a clown, and act hilariously just to bring joy to their dismal situation. Patch also loved to help sick people live their fantasies. To get an elderly woman to eat, he filled a portable swimming pool with pasta. The woman's fantasy was to swim in a pool of linguine. "Whatever it takes, by all means necessary," could be his slogan. To bring some joy, hope, and honor to others was his utmost desire.

Like Patch Adams, you too can realize that *a merry heart does good like a medicine!*

3. People may doubt what you say, but they will always believe what you do.

I had the honor of speaking at school assemblies in the great southern state of Louisiana. (Man, I love gumbo. Eat it twice a day, no joke!)

For two weeks, I traveled in almost every region of the state. I spoke at 20 high schools to approximately 10,000 students. I will never forget meeting Mr. Richards. He was the school custodian at one of the high schools where I addressed 1000 freshmen, sophomores, and juniors.

Mr. Richards was a true servant. He more than accommodated every need I had. He went to such lengths to service the program, even climbing to the top of the bleachers to open windows and ventilate the 90-degree gym. He was extremely polite; every other word was "yes sir, no sir, thank you, you're welcome." In all he did, Mr. Richards always had a pleasant attitude.

When the program was over, I gave him a signed copy of one of my books. He was so grateful. Then he went on to tell me how much he had enjoyed the program and that, earlier in his life, he was a drug addict and dealer. I told him my program that day was such a success because he (Mr. Richards) had been faithful to his call, that he did his job wholeheartedly and made my work much easier.

By the time we finished talking, we both had tears in our eyes. Mr. Richards may not receive all the accolades he deserves because our society often recognizes people only by their status. But I consider him to be one of the greatest of all. Why? He does his job with his whole heart. He asks for nothing in return. Mr. Richards is sincerely a man of character whose actions speak more loudly than words.

4. People feel honored to receive praise and appreciation.

After a horrible record at the beginning of the season, the New York Giants turned it around and finished its 1998 NFL season in a strong position, just barely missing the playoffs. At the end of the team's last game, I walked up to the head coach Jim Fassel and introduced myself. I told him how proud I felt because the Giants finished the season so well.

I can't tell you how much he appreciated my words. He said "Thank You" with great sincerity and was reluctant to let go of my outstretched hand. Many columnists, broadcasters, and fans had criticized the Giant's performance for months, so I know Coach Fassel felt especially honored to receive the praise and appreciation for leading his team's turnaround.

Why does our society set the tone for people to be critical? Why is it so hard to focus on the positive? Remember the phrase, "If you have nothing nice to say, don't say anything at all." Imagine if the majority of people lived by this as a core philosophy, what a happier world this could be!

5. Character can be developed through examples anytime, anywhere.

One day, I was traveling through an airport with my seven-year-old son Alec when we stopped to use the men's room. Before Alec could sit down, I had to clean the disgusting toilet seat that was splattered with urine. I just wanted to shout, "Hey, mister, you forgot to pick up the toilet seat."

It took me several minutes to clean up what could have taken someone several seconds of prevent, but it gave me the opportunity to explain to Alec the importance of thinking about others in a situation like this.

Alec watched my every move. He also saw me picking up paper off the bathroom floor and said, "Daddy, why are you picking up that paper? You didn't throw it on the floor."

I replied that we all need to chip in to keep our world a cleaner place. Several days later, I saw the result of this example. While participating in a church softball game, I noticed Alec picking up empty soda cans and throwing them in the garbage. The lesson paid off.

6. The price of greatness is responsibility.

I've been a major sports fan all my life and believe that professional athletes in the limelight have a responsibility to their fans...especially the younger ones. Whether the players like it or not, children look up to them as heroes and role models. They set a powerful example.

Because of this power, I'm not a big fan of today's professional sports practices. Though many players play for the love of the game, there are others who act less than responsibly. Look at contract re-negotiations as an example. It doesn't seem like a person's word or contract or signature means anything. How does an athlete have the nerve to sign a long-term contract for a certain number of dollars, then somewhere down the line, decide not to HONOR that contract until the team re-negotiates a new or better one? It seems that what the athlete's signature really mean this: "I am committed to this team (even though I signed a five year contract) until I feel I am worth more and should have a new contract drawn up. If my demands are not met, I will sit out/hold out until you re-negotiate my contract."

Could you imagine walking up to your boss and saying you will not continue to do your job until he or she re-negotiates and gives a better deal? If you follow the lead of certain pro athletes, you may quickly hear, "Hit the road Jack and don't you come back no more." The point is, be TRUE to your word.

7. Valuing principles before privileges builds character.

I would love to see sports fans put in as much effort into bettering the world as they do into supporting favorite sports teams. On the news recently, I heard that when the New York Yankees baseball team made it into the playoffs, fans waited in line for two to three days just to buy tickets to one baseball game.

How long will people wait in lines to help someone, to volunteer their time to a charitable organization, or to feed the hungry? Could you imagine if a line formed around Yankee Stadium just to go to church? Wow. How quickly people spend hundreds of dollars on entertainment but give only pennies to those in trouble. Certainly many people do their part, but if *everyone* did more, this world would be a much greater place to live.

8. Character may be manifested in the great moments, but it is *made* in the small ones!

One of my favorite speakers is a middle-aged, dynamic woman named Joyce Meyers. She is awesome! People love Joyce because she is down to earth and speaks their language.

Joyce motivates and ministers to millions of people worldwide, but she didn't arrive at her present status overnight. She constantly shares her heart and makes herself vulnerable to her listeners. She loves to talk about her "supermarket days" and how she had to be "faithful in the LITTLE before she could be ruler over much."

For example, she talks about loading groceries from a cart into her car and realizing how strongly she felt about her responsibility of returning the cart to the "Return Your Carts Here" area in the parking lot.

She shares another story about grocery shopping on a limited budget and the times she would reach the checkout counter with more groceries than money. Joyce knew it was wrong to leave the excess groceries at the checkout, so she would painstakingly return every item to its proper place.

How many times do you leave the cart one inch from someone else's car and don't take the 10 seconds to return it to its proper place? If there is no special place for carts, are you really expected to put them back in front of the store? YES!!!!!!!! When you shop, how many times do you see ground beef in the cereal isle, or candy in the soap department? What do you do?

Resolve to put things back where they belong. You see, it is all about being faithful and responsible doing the LITTLE things. This is where character begins.

Question, Activities & Exercises

Ask these questions to yourself, then discuss them with a friend.

Being a Servant:

Do you do regular chores at home?

Do you take responsibility for improving your home, school, church, and community?

List some ways that you can become even more of a servant to your family, friends, neighbors.

Stewardship:

What portion of your own money do you set aside to help others?

Which benevolent causes do you feel most passionate about?

Do you give your money and time even when you do not receive credit for doing so?

How do you volunteer your time to make a difference? Do you have more time that could be spent helping others?

List some ways your time and energy could be put to use to help others who are not as fortunate as you.

Integrity:

Are you true to your word?

Have you ever had plans with someone, only to get a better invitation from someone else? Did you feel tempted to lie to get out of the first invitation? Explain what you did.

Have you ever been the victim of dishonesty? Explain.

Have you ever been in situations that you not been true to your word? Explain. If you felt compelled to lie, how did it feel deep down inside?

List some ways that you feel you can improve your character to be a better leader.

About Bobby Petrocelli

Through his organization 10 Seconds, Inc., Bobby is on a mission to reach out and bring faith, hope and love, while teaching the power of decision making. Bobby's riveting story of how he triumphed over tragedy captivates audiences of all ages and backgrounds. His unforgettable programs inspire people to lead lives full of passion, hope, and forgiveness! He is the author of a best selling book TRIUMPH OVER TRAGEDY and has co-authored two other books in the TEEN POWER Series. Bobby's greatest loves are his faith, family and friends. Bobby is truly an inspiration to all!

10 Seconds, Inc.
P.O. Box 923, Bellport, NY 11713
Toll Free: 800-547-7933
Email: tseconds@aol.com • Web Site: www.10seconds.org

chapter 10

Responsibility

By John Crudele

The Link to Personal Freedom

LEAD NOW
or Step Aside!

Responsibility

By John Crudele

The Link to Personal Freedom

C an you think of a defining moment in your life? It could be a discovery made, a lesson learned, a tragedy avoided or endured. It may be a painful moment of accountability or a joyful moment of validation. These experiences, coupled with your responses to them, help shape who you are today.

One of my defining moments happened one day in the eighth grade. That's when I learned a unique lesson about responsibility from Mr. Byers, my history, government and homeroom teacher.

Mr. Byers had one eye. When he served during World War II, a bullet had entered through the eye socket and exited behind his ear. Consequently, he had a glass eye on one side and a real eye on the other. You never messed around in Mr. Byers' class, because one eye was always looking forward while the other eye would move around—and I couldn't always remember which was which.

On that afternoon at the Central Junior High gym, our principal Dr. Eilts asked us all to please rise for the Pledge of Allegiance. We obliged, and I stood with my buddies against the railing on the upper deck.

We began in unison, "I pledge allegiance to the…" and my buddy next to me said "flag" a little louder than I did. I figured I could be louder than that. So I belted out "of the United States of America." He added "and to the Republic…" I said louder still "for which it stands." Then I yelled "one nation under God!" He shouted back "indivisible!"

We just kept volleying the words back and forth with more and more lungpower when Mr. Byers ever so quietly asked us to come in after school.

"It's the way you guys were saying the pledge," he calmly explained after we gave him baffled looks.

"But we were saying the pledge," we defended.

"It was the way you were saying the pledge," he pointed out. "Come in after school." That was clearly the end of the discussion.

After school, Mr. Byers asked us to sit in the front row of his empty classroom. That sunny afternoon, he didn't go to the chalkboard. He didn't open a government or history book. He didn't look at a lesson plan.

Instead, Mr. Byers stood in front of us and silently looked into our eyes. Then, from the depths of his heart—in a loving, teacherly way—he reamed us up one side, across the top, and down the other. In that brief after-school session, he taught us respect for the flag, respect for the country, and respect for those for whom he nearly gave up his life. Some were people not yet born—people like us. Slowly, it became obvious he had undertaken a great responsibility to ensure our freedom—a freedom we had taken for granted.

"For America to experience true freedom—I recommend that the Statue of Liberty on the East Coast be supplemented by a Statue of Responsibility on the West," said Viennese psychologist and Holocaust survivor Viktor Frankl. "In fact," he added, "freedom is in danger of degenerating into mere arbitrariness unless it is lived in terms of responsibleness."

No wonder Mr. Byers was annoyed. He saw us enjoying the benefits of a free country but showing little respect toward one of its most important symbols. At that time, we perceived freedom as a right and responsibility with a sense of limitation and burden. Yet, in reality, responsibility creates the key link with personal freedom in many areas of life.

Responsibility is a quality involving self control, dependability and commitment whereby individuals accept the impact their actions have upon themselves and others. Let's take a closer look at how being more responsible can positively affect your relationships, your reputation, and your habits.

Resilient Relationships

"Friendship is the ability of two people to see the same truth and spend their lives supporting each other in its pursuit." When late British writer and professor C. S. Lewis expressed this thought, he implied that, as two people move toward the same truth, they naturally grow toward each other. Usually, the closer you are to others, the more you want what's best for them, long term. That takes responsibility.

However, when various issues trouble relationships—be they romantic or platonic—many choose to place blame instead of shouldering responsibility. For instance, you may make excuses for bad behavior because of earlier negative experiences. As a child, you may have indeed been a victim. Yet, as an adult, you become a volunteer if you choose to remain in unhealthy situations and don't take responsibility to face your past and to grow.

While the past may explain current behaviors, it doesn't excuse irresponsible choices. So if you are able to explain why something is happening—for instance, you don't trust a friend because your parents never trusted you—then you already have a head start on taking responsibility and doing something to change. If you are able to post blame, then you are able to do something about it.

Remember, blame looks backward at the past while responsibility looks forward to the future. When you hear someone complaining or blaming, they are simply not yet ready to become more responsible about that situation.

To gain more insight about the responsibility you do or do not take in relationships, consider the patterns you tend to follow. If you see an unhealthy pattern in your relationships—for instance, dating abusive people—it's probably not about the people you choose to date. It's probably more about you and the reasons you choose to be attracted to this type of person.

Recently, a student came up for counseling after I spoke at her school. Laura shared with me the tragedy of being date raped—something that had happened to her on three occasions over a period of several years.

Everyone knows that rape is wrong, and that "no" means "no." Still, to help Laura properly heal from those traumas, we needed to look more closely at patterns in her relationships. We decided that if she would take responsibility to address her conscious and unconscious needs and beliefs—with the help of a counselor—she could heal her past hurts. Consequently, Laura's attraction to potentially abusive situations will diminish, and her risk for future abuse will decrease as well.

On a less serious note, some people habitually get their feelings hurt by irresponsibly giving their heart away. Are you one of them? If so, you will continue facing that type of disappointment. Or, you can perform a quick "relationship inventory" and take more responsibility over your love life.

For instance, first realize that your fantasies will always be more attractive than your reality. That's why love at first sight is always perfect. It is totally absent of reality, so it's about your dream—it's not really about the other person at all.

Second, since love is a choice, you can choose to be more responsible about how you direct your romantic attention. If behaviors like dating abusive individuals or "falling in love" with a fantasy are not serving you well, grant yourself permission to change and make healthier choices.

Keep in mind that unhealthy patterns in relationships often reflect something in your conditioned beliefs about yourself that need addressing. If you don't give yourself the time and energy to change to something more positive—if you irresponsibly continue—then you will repeat unhappy scenarios of unrealistic expectations and disappointments over and over. I often tell students that craziness is going out on Friday and Saturday night and expecting different results from doing the same things. Yet, by taking responsibility for your issues—with professional help if necessary—you can change your unhealthy patterns.

A Reliable Reputation

Besides enhancing your one-on-one relationships, developing a history of acting responsibly will earn you the good reputation of being trustworthy. Of course, winning the trust of others takes time, yet it can be lost in a second. Though all can be forgiven, once broken, trust is seldom instantly re-established. However, by taking responsibility for your choices and actions, you can protect and build your reputation as a trustworthy person.

Consider my friend Bob who buys, develops, and sells businesses. He has assembled a management team that he trusts and that move with him from business to business. Because he trusts that his team is responsible for the results he seeks, Bob can better predict outcomes and manage his investment risks.

Likewise, the management team trusts Bob. They find security in his understanding of their time-tested ability to achieve results. Together, both parties have made it their responsibility to develop a mutual reputation of trustworthiness. When Bob focused on responsible leadership, his business grew. He learned early that while management is about what you do, leadership is about who you are.

How much people share with you—or how much you listen to what others share—depends on the level of respect between the two parties. In this sense, gaining influence has little to do with position or authority. The highest form of influence—be it in high school, college or business—involves respect.

Respect develops in this order of importance. Initially, you may oblige someone because of his or her position. Then you may connect with them more as your relationship grows. Next, if consistent, positive results come from that relationship, you'll appreciate them. Ultimately, you'll respect and trust them for who they are.

When I speak in schools across the U.S. and internationally, I ask the students who they trust enough to share their issues and problems. In each setting, I will invariably hear the same name over and over, and this indicates whom they most respect. You could be the class president or captain of a team or club. But your ability to lead will be based on the responsibility you have shown and, subsequently, the respect your peers have for you. Young or old, most people are attracted to honest, authentic, responsible individuals.

Think of the people you know. Whom do you trust to follow through on what they say? Whom would you call in an emergency? When tasks are being assigned on a leadership project, whom do you count on, and whom are you a little apprehensive about? Whom do you know will rationalize or make excuses later, and whom will follow-through on his or her responsibilities? Who will get the task done—no matter what? Whose response would you bet your reputation or your life on? Quite simply, whom do you trust? Are you someone others can respect and trust?

Always remember that maintaining a trustworthy reputation is one of the greatest assets in life—one developed through diligent, responsible action. To develop this characteristic, simply say what you are going to do, and do what you say consistently over time.

Time-Tested Habits

"Be certain that time is your friend." That is one on my favorite Crudele-isms. Why? No matter what, time will pass. The trick is taking enough responsibility to make sure time passes in your favor.

If, for example, you borrow money from a lender, that lender will more than likely charge you interest. (Your parents might represent the possible exception.) You will pay interest until you pay that lender back in full. So, in this case, time is not your friend. Time costs you cash!

However, if you keep a savings account, time works for you. Each day you keep money in the bank or invested elsewhere, you will earn interest. One dollar saved each day for 60 years, earning ten percent interest, will accrue to $1.2 million. Wow! Therefore, taking responsibility of your finances means avoiding or reducing debt while increasing savings.

Keep in mind that habits, be they financial or otherwise, will defend themselves until either their death or yours—whichever comes first. Of course, healthy habits—like regularly bathing, brushing your teeth and studying—can be left alone. But, if you have unhealthy habits, address them directly for the best chance to change.

A student once complained to me that his coach had kicked him off the team for consuming alcohol. I asked Todd what the discipline policy was regarding drinking. At that moment it became clear that he had kicked himself off the team. By acting irresponsibly, Todd had damaged his reputation and compromised his freedom to participate. The coach was just the bearer of the bad news.

Similarly, in the classroom, teachers do not fail students. Students fail themselves when they lack the responsibility and discipline necessary to study. Many students in this category seem to have become comfortable being uncomfortable. Furthermore, they may have beliefs filled with rationalizations that blame others to justify their situation and defend their habits.

Habits can be good or bad. They can enslave and entrap you or they can propel you to great good and accomplishment and free you to become the person you are capable of being. Leadership trainer Rick Loy says, "Habits are the small choices and actions you make each day that eventually define your life." How are you defining yours?

Defining Moments

Are you responsibly making good choices today? Everybody faces challenging circumstances and responds to them in either a healthy or unhealthy fashion. The difference depends on whether you take responsibility to plan your response and do something about it, or whether you rationalize an irresponsible reaction. In either case, your freedom to succeed in life will be established by how you manage your response to circumstances and plan your future attitudes, beliefs and behaviors.

What stands are you going to take regarding your relationships, reputation and habits? Will you be able to live with the results of your choices five, ten, or even 15 years from now? Begin by taking responsibility for your thoughts, feelings, and actions. Let this be your defining moment! As the one-eyed Mr. Byers taught me during that awkward after-school session, your response is always your responsibility and your link to personal freedom.

Questions, Activities & Exercises

A. What does "taking responsibility" mean to you?

B. List the qualities and characteristics of people you trust and respect.

1. _____   6. _____

2. _____   7. _____

3. _____   8. _____

4. _____   9. _____

5. _____   10. _____

Are these traits that you have? _____

List three traits you could improve upon.

1. _____

2. _____

3. _____

With whom can you spend time to help strengthen these traits? (mentors)

_____   _____   _____

C. List the names of your three best friends, the last three people you've dated or hung out with more than five times, and three people you do not respect.

List some qualities you admire and respect in each of these relationships.

1. _____   6. _____

2. _____   7. _____

3. _____   8. _____

4. _____   9. _____

5. _____   10. _____

List some qualities you dislike and do not respect in each of these relationships.

1. _____   6. _____

2. _____   7. _____

3. _____   8. _____

4. _____   9. _____

5. _____   10. _____

These lists reflect what you value in friendships and indicate what, for better or for worse, attracts you to various relationships.

D. Name three habits you would like to change and why.

1. _____

2. _____

3. _____

What choices can you make to stop practicing these habits?

1. _____   6. _____

2. _____   7. _____

3. _____   8. _____

4. _____   9. _____

5. _____   10. _____

Action Point: Each day, practice the qualities you admire in others, and strive to avoid or replace those qualities that you disrespect. As you develop positive characteristics in your life, you will tend to attract relationships and opportunities that reflect those values.

About John Crudele

A compelling speaker for school, conference and community events! For 15 years John's humorous insights and powerful delivery style propelled him to deliver more than 3500 programs to over a million youth, teachers and parents internationally, to be a frequent TV guest and host his own national radio talk show. With compassion and conviction John addresses sensitive youth and family topics and destructive societal issues. Audiences are moved by his stories, attracted to his authenticity, and challenged by his honesty. John's books include *Making Sense of Adolescence: How to Parent From the Heart.* and contributions to the *TEEN POWER* series.

John Crudele Productions
6100 Green Valley Drive, Suite 120, Minneapolis, MN 55438
612-835-0008   fax 612-835-0004   Toll Free: 800-899-9543
Email: JCSpeak@aol.com • Web Site: www.johncrudele.com

chapter 11

Sportsmanship

By Tony Schiller

"Mastering the Internal Victory"

Sportsmanship

By Tony Schiller

"Mastering the Internal Victory"

*"It is far better to deserve honors and not receive them
than to receive them and not be deserving."*
– Albert Einstein

I n ancient times, one of the most popular athletic
competitions was the long distance foot race. Back
then, the stakes were pretty high. Victory earned
fame and fortune, while defeat usually led to a slow
and painful death ceremony. Thankfully, we've come
a long way and most of us no longer take sports or
competition quite so seriously.

If you get past the penalty for losing, you'll find a lot
to admire in ancient competition... in particular, their
high regard for sportsmanship. It was a time when
nothing was worse than living as a known "cheat."

The system worked well and made for some good entertainment. That is, until the athletes united, declared
free agency, and formed their own league that competed for medals instead of lives. The new league
gained popularity, sold tickets, and made heroes out
of their big stars.

Life was good.

However, it seems that once death was taken out of the equation, the idea of a noble defeat lost its luster. This was especially true after athletes saw how shiny and choice the medals were. Winning those medals, even if it meant stepping on your competitor's toes, soon became every young warrior's obsession. In no time at all, the time-honored tradition that had revered exemplary sportsmanship was lost.

Now you can bring it back.

About 2500 years later, competition in your school goes far beyond the foot race. It includes dozens of activities—in and out of sports. How prevalent are "win-at-all-cost" attitudes in your activities? Is sportsmanship still alive and well at your school? Which is valued more by your coaches and school at large, sportsmanship or winning?

Define Sportsmanship

Let's start by defining sportsmanship. These few descriptions come to mind: playing fair, being a good loser, and eliminating cheating, taunting, trash-talking, and dirty or unfair play.

I want to go beyond those initial definitions to really challenge your beliefs about competition, not just in athletics but in all aspects of your life. Because even if you don't participate in sports, being in competition is a fact of life.

Think about it. As a leader, you compete every time you try out for a role in a play, enter a speech contest, run for student government, challenge yourself for better grades, or interview for a job. Heck, you may even have to compete to get a date for the prom.

Love it or hate it, for you'll enter into competitive situations for the rest of your life. This is even more true for you, a leader, who's unwilling to watch from the sidelines.

Approach with an Open Mind

Before we go any further, consider these questions:

- Do you fire yourself up by getting mentally psyched to pound or even destroy the competition?

- Do you think of your competition as the enemy?

- Do you believe that too much attention to sportsmanship only weakens one's resolve to be an outstanding competitor?

If you answered yes to those questions, then let me persuade you to approach this topic with an open mind concerning what I am about to share. In the end, you might have a change of heart and see how the opposite is actually true... that you could be stronger vs. weaker and achieve more of your natural potential. It also makes competition more fun and a lot less stressful.

Race of All Races

The following story about a long distance foot race in not-quite-ancient times forms the basis for my approach to sportsmanship.

During my collegiate racing days, Daryl Henderson was our team's star and the most unassuming champion I've ever known. By contrast, his main challenger, Dave Renneison, loved the limelight and was as cocky and flashy as they come.

Dave, nicknamed "Reni" (pronounced Ren-eye), was tall and lean and glided like a gazelle. Daryl hardly seemed a match. His short, twiggy legs needed to go into overdrive to stay near guys like Reni.

Just the same, it was Daryl whom Reni feared the most. He knew Daryl was a master of managing and controlling pain—that he had an uncanny ability to block out every thought that was contrary to going faster. All of this led to his greatness and a finishing kick that was nothing short of amazing.

When the two All Americans had their final collegiate cross-country showdown, Reni was the only runner given a prayer of beating Daryl. So following a simple strategy—get far ahead and start praying—Reni attacked early and quickly left everyone in his dust. Even Daryl appeared out of contention, especially when his attempts to catch up only lost more ground.

Reni was running as if possessed and not about to slow down. His huge lead grew and we all conceded the race to him… that is, all of us except for Daryl. He said that Reni's courage inspired him to get back into the race. And get back into it he did.

Reaching deep, Daryl began to fly and closed much of the gap. Impressed as we were by his gutsy charge, we believed it was too little too late. But then with a quarter mile to go, Daryl hit the afterburners and really lit up the course. Shockingly, he suddenly had a shot to take the race at the wire.

And then it happened.

Running for his life, Reni made a blunder for the ages when he overran the final turn. All Daryl had to do was turn right and waltz down the homestretch to repeat as conference champion.

What Would You Do?

Now put yourself in Daryl's shoes. What would you do if this scenario unfolded for you in the heat of battle? Would you go out of your way to help Reni, or would you capitalize on his mistake?

I've asked many high school and collegiate athletes—usually team captains—to discuss this same question during the sportsmanship workshops I've conducted. The typical responses are:

"Your first responsibility is to your team so you've gotta take his mistake as a gift."

"I agree. I'd feel badly for Reni but..."

"I wouldn't. It's his own fault—he screwed up."

"Plus, he's the enemy. Why would you help him? He sure as heck isn't going to help you."

"Well, I probably wouldn't be as proud of winning that way, but I could live with myself."

After further explaining the first rule of cross-country is to "know the course"—adding that Reni had won on this course before—the attendees showed even more resolve:

"That's the breaks."

"It's a great lesson for him. Next time he'll know the course."

"Yep, I'd take the gift and enjoy the victory."

The Rest of the Story

But here's the rest of the story... Daryl didn't take the "gift." Without hesitation, he chased off course—putting a sure victory and our team's score at risk—all the while shouting to his confused rival. When Reni finally turned back, Daryl waited for him so the two could rejoin the course together—now both tied for 4th place.

Reni was emotionally thunderstruck and never recovered. He faded badly while Daryl somehow reloaded. And to everyone's amazement, he out-sprinted the new leaders. Afterwards, his victory was "all the buzz." Even Reni couldn't believe what Daryl had done for him. He summed up what many of us were thinking, "Man, had that been me, I woulda' said, 'Thanks dude! See ya'."

Important Lesson

But Daryl rejected the praises. Explaining to me why it was a tainted victory, he taught me an important lesson about sportsmanship.

"Tony, what would it have proven had I turned the corner without helping Reni... that I can win when there's no one to beat?" I countered, "Yea, but he wouldn't have helped you; he said so himself." "Maybe not, but we don't know that for sure," he said. "Besides, I don't live my life based on what others do."

"OK, that makes sense. So explain to me why, after doing the right thing, you're still bummed out about the race?" I asked. His answer blew me away. "It was the perfect race. Both of us were so ON. We pushed each other beyond belief and it was the best feeling. But then Reni went off course. Now I'll never know how it would have turned out."

What's Behind His Philosophy

Let's look further into his philosophy. What was the source of Daryl's best feeling? Was it dependent on his winning? Did the threat of losing lessen or increase that feeling? What can you take from that?

Did you also notice that he said, "*I'll* never know how it would have turned out," not, "*we'll* never know...?" Think about what that means. His primary concern wasn't for others to recognize him as the best but to know in his heart that he reached his highest potential. He saw the gesture as the least he could do for Reni who ran such a courageous race. He also said had he taken the easy victory, living with himself would have been tough.

Remember the Einstein quote on *being deserving*?

What disheartened Daryl then, and probably still does today, is that he never got to run the homestretch with Reni. He recognized how rare the competitive opportunity was, and that it had been lost.

Daryl's Legacy

Do you share this philosophy? If not, think about this... how do you suppose Daryl is remembered by coaches and athletes today? How would his legacy be different had he taken the easy victory? What if he also mocked Reni, just to rub salt in his wounds? Hopefully, such poor sportsmanship is rare today.

Of course, you might argue that Daryl's attitude is a little extreme as well. But Daryl proved that being a class act *doesn't* diminish one's competitive spirit. History shows that records get broken and champions are forgotten, but legacies live on. What do legacies mean to you?

Let's reconsider the definition of sportsmanship. If competition is a given, think of sportsmanship as the *attitude you bring to competition.* It goes far beyond whether you compete fairly and win without gloating. **Sportsmanship is about balancing a strong desire to win with a personal commitment to be ethical.**

Deserving to Win

Einstein's quote at the start of this chapter is such an awesome approach to competition. It shifts the entire goal from an emphasis on winning to an emphasis on *deserving* to win.

How do you adopt this approach to competition? By showing *respect* to your teammates, coaches, advisors, and yes, even your competitors. By modeling high *integrity* in your effort, commitment, and loyalty to your team. And, finally, by *celebrating* your outcomes. Win or lose, how do you accept the results? It's all about the manner in which you represent your school—inside and outside of competition.

Has this chapter helped you gain a greater perspective on sportsmanship? How has your attitude changed? What stands out as a concept you want to take action on now to help your team or group or school?

You'll have to muster your courage to take action. It's not easy to bring up these issues with coaches, teammates, friends, and family. It's even tougher to make a stand no matter how much resistance you face. But the pay-off will be more than worth it. In the end, you'll be *deserving of winning*.

Questions, Activities & Exercises

Below are several scenarios regarding sportsmanship and teamwork that pose some tough questions to discuss with your teammates. See how you can set standards for handling these situations.

- It's play-off time and your captains decide the whole team should shave heads for team unity. Two players refuse and a controversy ensues. How can the conflict be resolved? Is their refusal a betrayal to the team? Is it OK to force them to shave—for the good of the team?

• A freshman is chosen over your best friend—a senior—for the lead role in the school play. Your friend feels bitter and persuades other cast members to disrupt the production by making life miserable for the newcomer. You feel for your friend but know he/she is out of line. How do you respond? What do you think about an advisor or coach picking an underclassman over a senior?

• Your coach shows favoritism to you and a few star players while punishing the rest of the team for little reason. You know it's unfair and that some kids are considering quitting. What can you do?

• When first in high school, you were taken to a park, tied to a tree and left there until rescued by a jogger. You didn't like it but knew it was the price of gaining acceptance. Now that you're a senior, do you consider it payback time? Is this tradition just a part of growing up? Is it OK to dish it out as long as no one gets hurt and it's not too humiliating? Who decides what is or isn't too humiliating? As a leader, how can you break the cycle of hazing?

• Several of your teammates started using anabolic steroids and have seen big results. You know they are illegal, unethical, and have unhealthy side effects, but you have been told it's your only hope for getting a college scholarship. They say your use will merely level the playing field. Does the end justify the means? What substances, legal or not, are you willing to take to achieve your goals? Will you be proud to tell your kids how you achieved your success?

- A teammate is berated after almost every contest by his/her mom/dad. Despite your teammate's denial of the problem, you believe the abuse is causing him/her severe distress. What options do you and your teammates have to help? Is it your problem?

- Your swim team leads the conference meet until your rival pulls off an upset by sweeping the top three places in the second to last race. But a parent notices the three swimmers had switched from their assigned lanes and demands they be disqualified. Before filing a protest and winning the title on a technicality, your coach puts it to the team for a vote. How will you have him/her handle it?

- A teammate starts performing better than ever. The only problem is he/she plays the same position (or instrument) as you. How do you handle the challenge? Do you welcome it or see it as a threat and hope for his/her failing?

- You catch several of your teammates drinking at a party. As team captain and a non-user, their stupidity and lack of commitment upsets you. How do you handle it? Does their importance to the team alter your actions? If so, how?

- You recently lost a heated contest with a conference rival. As members of the visiting team, you and your teammates were treated with total disrespect by the opponent's fans. The big rematch is tonight and you've learned that several students from your school are looking for revenge. In your role as captain, do their plans concern you, or do you believe the situation is out of your control?

About Tony Schiller

As a kid, Tony dreamed of being a big league ballplayer. That dream died on his 15th birthday when he was cut for the 7th straight year. But instead of quitting, he started running and has now won over 150 races including 3 triathlon world championships. As an inspiring storyteller, Tony brings out the leadership attributes of his audiences by drawing on lessons learned during his struggling young years and from those gained in life as a professional athlete. Since 1990, he's presented at hundreds of k-12 schools and at leadership and sportsmanship conferences on "how to be a BreakAway Leader."

BreakAway Motivation
6580 Troendle Circle, Chanhassen, MN 55317
612-474-3278   fax 612-474-4527   Toll Free: 800-863-3278
Email: Tony@TalkingTony.com • Web Site: www.TalkingTony.com

chapter 12

Truth and Honor

By Jeff Yalden

When All Else Fails, the Person of Truth and Honor Prevails

LEAD NOW
or Step Aside!

Truth and Honor

By Jeff Yalden

When All Else Fails, the Person of Truth and Honor Prevails

These days, you hear a lot of talk about truth and honor, but the definitions are not always the same. However, it has been my experience that these two words go hand in hand and are qualities that serve as the backbone of true leadership.

To fully understand the meaning of truth and honor, we can't simply look in the dictionary. We need to look at real life examples of people in difficult situations and the choices they've made. Acting with truth and honor is not always easy, but it is always right. I should know; I learned the hard way.

In March of 1994, I was stationed in Camp Lejuene, NC, only 40 days from my honorable discharge date in the United States Marine Corps, and my record was spotless. I had labored for years to become a Marine of respect and distinction, and I was proud of my service record. One weekend, I was standing guard with another Marine, Sergeant Rushing.

I had just completed my 24-hour duty and I was due to be relieved at 8:00 a.m. (0800) Sunday morning by Sgt. Rushing. Eight o'clock came and went, and Sgt.

Rushing did not arrive. What was I to do? He was AWOL (Absent With Out Leave) and I could not leave my post until properly relieved of all duties and responsibilities. If I called the Officer in Charge (OOD), Sgt. Rushing would have been in a lot of trouble. He probably would be arrested, reduced from Sergeant to Private, and possibly dishonorably discharged from the military.

QUESTION: *If you were in my shoes (or boots, as the case may be), what would you have done?*

What I did seemed right at the time, but it turned out to be one of the worst mistakes of my life. I chose to stay on guard and not let anyone know Sgt. Rushing was missing. Everything was going along fine until noon, when the OOD asked where Sgt. Rushing was. I told the officer Sgt. Rushing had gone to chow. The officer accepted my answer and told me to have Sgt. Rushing call him upon his return.

Covering for Sgt. Rushing was the easy and natural way to avoid conflict, but I soon realized that I had compromised my own honor with the OOD. I became scared, but didn't know how to get out of the lie I had just told. When the OOD returned later that afternoon, I lied again and said Sgt. Rushing had gone to get a haircut. Again, compromised my own honor by lying, and instead of getting me out of the jam, it only pulled me in deeper.

QUESTION: *At this point, should I have called the OOD and explained the situation, or continued to try to cover it up in hopes that it would all go away?*

Had I chosen at this point to go to the OOD with the truth and admit I was covering for Sgt. Rushing, I may have gotten a lecture, but I would have freed myself from the situation. Then it would have been between the OOD and Sgt. Rushing. Instead, concerned for my friend—and not wanting to be a "rat"—I continued the deception, hoping everything would just magically smooth itself out. Perhaps I could have gotten away from the lie, but after a restless weekend, I came to realize that I couldn't get away from myself. My conscience was killing me!

On Monday morning when I logged out, I decided to go to the Staff Sergeant and tell the truth. At this point, I believed the Staff Sergeant would talk to Sgt. Rushing and handle the situation without incident. Instead, before I knew it, I was in the Commanding Officer's (CO's) office in a lot of trouble!

As it turned out, I didn't lose my rank. I did, however, have the words "lack of integrity" and "lied to an officer" written in my Service Record Book. This was the first—and only—blemish ever to appear on my stellar Marine Corps career record. And I could have avoided the pain, worry, and embarrassment had I made the right choice from the beginning.

QUESTIONS: When *did I begin to lose my honor? At what point in this situation should I have spoken up and told the truth?*

Clearly, I made the wrong choice. I was dishonest to the OOD and the United States Marine Corps. By trying to cover for another Marine, I place myself in an uncomfortable position and put my honor on the line. To this day, I wonder if Sgt. Rushing was as concerned about my friendship and my career as I was about his. I seriously doubt it.

Situations like this test our truth and honor. That time, I failed. But since then, I've learned how important it is to *take time to think*. These are the four Ts taught in the Marine Corps to help one make the right choice in any situation. When you are put in a difficult spot where you need to make a difficult decision, always remember the four Ts—Take Time To Think.

Foundation of Truth and Honor

The other day, I asked a friend who teaches middle school English what he thought of when he considered the concepts of "truth" and "honor" as it applies to today's teens. He said he felt that, in today's society, many of our leaders and public figures, and sometimes people in our legal system, send the wrong messages to kids about living the truth and being honorable.

What messages, he asked, are kids today receiving when their leaders refuse to accept responsibility for their actions? The message being sent is that if you have the right lawyer, a lie can become the truth, and a person's honor is immaterial. Lying, infidelity, and even murder seem to fall by the wayside as the perpetrators hide behind professionally manufactured excuses. How can young people grow to become respectable leaders when many of today's high-profile leaders aren't demonstrating truth and honor with their own actions?

I believe young people should instead pattern their actions after those who *forged their own paths,* not *covered their own tracks.* They should look to true leaders like Dr. Martin Luther King, Jr., a pioneer of the Civil Rights Movement in the 1960s; Neil Armstrong, who boldly took the first steps on the moon; and Gandhi, the leader of India who freed his people from British colonial rule without the use of violence. These honorable people lived the truth even when it put their personal comfort—and even their life—on the line.

There are many others who have inspired us with their humanity through honor. Consider Oprah Winfrey, one of the best-known celebrities in the world, who commonly uses her talk show to ease racial tensions. She brings dignity to television by refusing to stoop to the tasteless level of other talk shows.

Former President of the United States Jimmy Carter is another example. After losing a second term bid for the presidency, he helped to form Habitat for Humanity, a non-profit organization that recruits people to build houses for low income Americans who would not otherwise be able to afford a home of their own.

You can always gain inspiration from Dr. Jonas Salk, who pioneered a cure for polio with the Salk vaccine. He gave up years of his life to research but he never gave up in his fight to save others.

What has made these people such dynamic leaders we respect and revere? There are many factors, but high on the list is the truth and honor they demonstrated. However, while they stand out as role models today, all the great leaders mentioned above are human. Like you, when they were young, they sat in classrooms, hung out with friends, played sports, and had arguments with their parents. They too made mistakes, told lies, and fell out of honor. But at some point in their lives, each of them made the conscious decision to live a life of truth and honor. And by the example they've set, each of these leaders had made an enormous difference in the world.

Being a leader is a tremendous responsibility because others will put their trust in you. You'll become a model showing others the right way to live and how to make good decisions. What you do and say, and *how* you do and say it sends messages about who you are and what you stand for. If dishonorable and untruthful, you will lose the respect of family, friends, and those who look to you for guidance.

As you know, actions speak louder than words. Leaders are given a sacred trust. A great leader can positively influence many lives, while a bad one can betray that trust and let people down in their times of need. But no leader ever failed by living a life of truth and honor.

TAKE TIME TO THINK:

Think about the great leaders I mentioned earlier. Then think about a teacher, friend, parent, or coach who has made a difference in your life by being there for you with compassion, understanding, and faith.

Why do you respect and admire these leaders? What is it about them that makes you want to emulate them? How do they exemplify truth and honor? How would you feel about them if you discovered they had lied to you?

Living the Honorable Life

No one can feel good about himself or herself if they are cheating, stealing, or doing wrong. The day a person awakens and does not respect the person staring back from the mirror, it is time for that person to change. Only those who accept responsibility and are accountable for their actions are able to look at their reflection and say, "I am a good, worthwhile person. People like and respect me."

When I was a coach, I tried to emphasize the importance of approaching life with truth and honor. This to me was far more important than winning a game.

I remember a situation where an athlete had $20 stolen from his wallet. I had an idea of who had taken it, and most everyone on the team suspected the same person. Knowing that this incident would eventually divide our team, I called a team meeting and brought up the facts. I then promised that, if the money were returned to the rightful owner, the matter would be closed. I wanted to give the young man who had stole the cash an opportunity to (TTTT) take time to think. I wanted him to reflect on what it meant to his self-respect, what it meant to our team, and how he had lowered himself and put his honor in jeopardy. I hoped he would choose to make the right decision and return the money.

Sure enough, the next day the money was returned. That evening, my phone rang and it was the young man who I had suspected on the other end. He apologized for what he had done, and then he thanked me for the opportunity to make things right. He had learned an incredible lesson that will serve him throughout his life.

Making Mistakes

Growing up is about making mistakes and learning from them. We all make poor choices from time to time, and this is to be expected. It is okay to fail—but it's never to okay to cover up our failures by cheating, lying, and manipulating the truth. I am convinced that the best leaders are those that have learned from their mistakes and gone on to help others avoid making the same mistakes.

It takes guts to own up to your mistakes. "Owning up" does not "make up" for the mistake, but it is the first step towards establishing honor. People will always respect a leader who has the courage to admit when they've been wrong or made an error. Likewise, people will loose confidence and trust in a leader who never admits to their mistakes and is instead always looking to place blame on someone else for something they themselves did.

I challenge you to always be truthful to yourself and others and act honorably. You can't be "kind of" truthful or "kind of" honest—just like you cannot be "kind of" pregnant; either you are or you aren't.

Live the truth and strive to be a leader in life. You'll always feel better about yourself when you choose the *difficult right* over the *easy wrong*.

This is the essence of truth and honor.

Questions, Activities & Exercises

You are the co-captain of the soccer team. At the beginning of the season, you made a pact with the other team members that no one would drink throughout the season. The night before Saturday's quarterfinal game, you go to party where beer is being served. As you glance around the room, you see that other co-captain and three of the best players from your team have violated the pact—and school rules—as they are all drinking beer. Telling on them will get them suspended and kicked off the team. It might also give you a reputation as a "rat." Not telling on them might mean they will play hung-over and jeopardize the team's chance of winning.

a. What is the honorable thing to do?

b. What is the right thing to do?

c. How would you handle the situation?

d. If the roles were switched and you were the one caught drinking, what would you expect the other captain/players to do?

e. Suppose you chose to remain quiet and the guilty players showed up, played well, and the team won. Is everything back to normal?

You are the number-two student in your class and you are taking the Pre-Calculus final exam. You have received reliable—but unproven information—that the number-one student in the class has managed to get the answers to the exam. When the results come back, your score is a 92, while the number-one student scored a 98 and kept you from overtaking their class ranking.

a. What is the honorable thing to do?

b. What is the easiest thing to do?

c. Would you say something and risk losing your reputation?

d. If you ignore it, how would you feel knowing you lost the number-one class ranking to the valedictorian whom you believe cheated?

e. Would your decision change if the college of your choice accepted the other student instead of you, based on these test results?

About Jeff Yalden

Jeff graduated 128 of 133 students, was rejected by 16 of 19 colleges and scored a whopping 610 on his SAT's. Yes, he was LD (Learned Differently), had a stutter, twitch, a bad attitude and a negative self-image. Jeff eventually became depressed and even suicidal. Through courage, faith, and hard work, he changed the course of his future. Jeff graduated, became Mr. New Hampshire Male America and a proud U.S. Marine. Today, he presents 300 programs annually, and has captivated audiences in 38 states. Visit his web site for information on his dynamic speeches, or to order audio and video tape programs.

Motivate by Jeff Yalden
1 Clocktower Place, Suite 419, Nashua, NH 03060
603-594-9371   fax 603-579-0325   Toll Free: 800-948-9289
Email: JeffYalden@aol.com • Web Site: www.JeffYalden.com

Part Three
Troubleshooting

Risk Taking

By Ellen Marie, M.S.

What's the Price of Taking Risks?

187

Risk Taking

By Ellen Marie, M.S.

What's the Price of Taking Risks?

S hortly after speaking to a high school group recently, one of the young men in the audience sent me an e-mail message. Instead of asking the usual questions about dating or how to figure out his girlfriend, he wrote:

"Hi Ellen. I really liked your talk at our school about dating and waiting until marriage for sex. I agree with all that. But pre-marital sex isn't my problem. I can't even get a date! You see, I have no real friends. What can I do to make friends? I'm really a nice person, but no one knows this because I can't seem to meet people."

Does that sound like anyone you know?

In my return e-mail, I explained that it takes two things to make friends: showing interest in others and taking risks. For instance, if that lonely student would risk getting involved in extra-curricular activities, he would both explore his interests and develop his talents while meeting others with similar interests. In this way, he could more than likely achieve his goal—finding friends.

Seems too simple, doesn't it? Of course, taking risks can be extremely challenging, but some risks are worth it. Do you agree?

Risk Taker or Risk Breaker?

Do you think you are a risk taker? If so, what kind of a risk taker are you? After all, there are healthy and unhealthy ways to take risks. I call the first group "risk takers" and the second group "risk breakers."

Risk takers choose healthy risks—risks that involve the possibility of moving to a higher level in sports, academics or another area that's important to them. In healthy risk-taking situations, even if the outcome doesn't turn out as expected, the risk taker will manage the loss and be fine.

On the other hand, risk breakers choose risks with the potential to harm themselves or others. In unhealthy risk-taking situations, things can get pretty scary if the outcome doesn't match the individual's expectation.

It's important to learn good ways to judge when a risk is healthy or unhealthy. Let's take a closer look at that decision process.

Risks That Kill

When the cost of the worst possible outcome outweighs the best possible benefit of taking a risk, I call that negative risk taking. In most cases, negative risk taking is easy to spot. Consider the following true stories.

Situation 1

Todd was a smart, popular student on campus who had a great future until one day in October 1998. His college buddies had dared him to swallow an entire bottle of caffeine pills. When he took them up on the dare, he took a negative risk and died that night from overdosing. He was just 20 years old.

Situation 2

It was a great day to celebrate the California sun, so a group of teens got together at a local water park to cool off and have some fun. But what started out as a game quickly got out of hand when 30 kids crammed together on a water slide in June 1997. Not surprisingly, they exceeded the structure's weight limit. The slide collapsed and sent everyone tumbling to the ground. The accident killed one girl and injured the others.

Situation 3

In December 1998, 16-year-old Brittney was four days away from getting her license. To celebrate that milestone, her parents had secretly bought her a car as a surprise present. However, before that day arrived, she risked accepting a ride home with a friend who had been drinking alcohol. Though she knew it was unsafe and her parents would be furious, she went anyway. Brittney must have rationalized that home wasn't far away and that just this one time everything would be OK.

Unfortunately, the driver sped around a turn, lost control and flipped the car. He walked away dazed, but

Brittney lay dead against the windshield. She never saw her family's shock and grief at her untimely death, but I saw it because her dad is my brother.

Discussion

1. Situation 1. Is the person who dared Jason responsible for the outcome of Jason's risk? Is Jason more or less responsible than the person who dared him?

2. Situation 2. How much responsibility should the teen who suggested cramming 30 people onto the water park slide assume? Is the water park at fault if they didn't post a sign warning that the slide would not hold 30 people?

3. Situation 3. Is the driver at fault, even if Brittney willingly got into his car?

Remember that risks have a ripple affect. When you take risks, those risks affect others in either positive or negative ways. In this sense, we are all "ripplers."

However, leaders create even more of a ripple effect and can either lead toward positive or negative situations through the risks they take. Consider leaders like Mother Teresa and Princess Diana vs. Adolf Hitler or a cult leader.

Are you a positive or negative "rippler?" Are your actions helping others feel good about themselves? Or do others feel worse about themselves after spending time with you? Are the risks you take helping or hurting yourself and others?

Risks That Thrill

I have always loved risks. As a child, I would jump off railroad bridges into water, flip off the high dive and race any boy on the playground. I was always challenging myself and getting an adrenaline high from taking risks to test my limits.

As I matured, I channeled my desire for risks into positive opportunities. I took classes from trampoline to tennis to tap dance. I joined clubs, attended Christian Bible studies, and went to camps. I participated in many sports, including ones people may consider risky such as white-water rafting, scuba diving, and skydiving.

However, some risks I won't take—risks like engaging in sex before marriage, driving drunk, or taking illegal drugs. I've decided that taking these risks aren't worth the reward.

To decide which risks are worth it, ask yourself if taking the risk can make you and others a better person. Obviously, healthy risks hold that potential. Unhealthy risks, on the other hand, could jeopardize or negatively change your life or the lives of others if the risk proves unsuccessful.

Healthy risks include trying out for a sport, drama club, band, or student council. Planning a fundraiser, doing a new volunteer activity, or entering a talent contest represent other positive risks.

Being a positive risk taker could also mean befriending someone who needs a friend, studying in a foreign country, interviewing for a job, asking for a date, finding a solution to a problem, admitting you are wrong, or resisting peer pressure that involves negative risk taking.

What are some healthy risks you would like to take?

Count the Cost

The best way to judge risks boils down to one question: "What do you have to lose?" If a little embarrassment or frustration comes from a risk that doesn't turn out the way you had hoped, then go for it! It's a healthy risk.

"You miss 100 percent of the shots you never take," says former NHL star Wayne Gretzky. Healthy risks deserve a try, while unhealthy risks don't. Again, unhealthy risks include drinking, driving drunk, using illegal drugs and having sex outside of marriage.

When I was the director of a Minneapolis-based crisis pregnancy center, I met many women who took risks in the latter category. When they took that risk, they mistakenly thought they controlled the outcome perfectly.

I don't remember her name, but one young woman's face is still clear to me. Beautiful with a big smile, she came into our crisis pregnancy center for a pregnancy test. She expressed confidence while saying she "knew" she wasn't pregnant because she always used condoms during sexual intercourse. However, the condom broke once and she wanted to be 100 percent sure she wasn't pregnant.

As we waited for the test results, she told me of her dream to become a lawyer. She had just graduated from college and had been accepted to the law school of her dreams. I told her I thought she would make a great lawyer.

Soon, the test results came back and she was shocked. The 22-year-old woman cried for a long time over the news of her pregnancy. "This was not supposed to happen," she said repeatedly.

Of course, the problem was not the pregnancy itself. The problem was that she took a risk, and she wasn't ready to deal with the possible outcomes.

Discussion

1. Was the woman not at fault for getting pregnant because she used a condom and it broke?

2. If she loved the father of the child and they were going to be married after she completed law school, would this change your opinion of the risk she took?

Emotional Risks

Not all risks involve typically risky behaviors. For instance, when I was in high school, I took a risk and befriended a classmate I'll call Tom. He was a loner, but I remember being nice to him. It wasn't difficult. I just asked him about his life with kindness. Some of my friends thought it was uncool to talk to those outside our group, but I didn't care. Tom was a good guy.

Years after graduation, I met Tom again after a class reunion. There, he told me I was the only person in our whole high school who had treated him with respect. He thanked me and explained how high school was painful for him—especially since he had a tough home life and no friends. He said if it weren't for my kindness, he may have committed suicide.

Later, Tom reached out to me in kindness. The man I thought I was going to marry had just dumped me and I was devastated. I felt confused, heartbroken, and hopeless. Tom called to encourage me. I realized then that by giving to others, if often comes back to you.

In this case, the ripple effect was positive. I took a risk when Tom needed me and, many years later, Tom took a risk when I needed him. This is what the ripple effect is all about.

Is there a Tom at your school who could benefit from your kindness? Maybe the person's name is Kaitlin, Brandon or Patty. Of course, you don't have to be best friends with everyone. Still, you can take an emotional risk and treat everyone—including those outside of group—with the respect they deserve.

Discussion

1. When is it an emotional risk to be a friend? Is it more or less a risk to befriend someone your friends don't like?

2. Why do you think people form cliques or select groups? Why is there a need to associate with one group of people more than others?

3. Is it normal to want to be closer friends with some people more than others?

4. Why do some groups identify with a color or symbol and hate others who don't share that identity?

Before taking a risk, consider the following questions:

1. Are you willing to live with all possible outcomes, including the worst things that could go wrong?

2. Do you think the others involved can accept all possible outcomes of the risk?

3. If you take the risk, will it help to achieve even better goals? For example, if you want to play football at your high school, you must first risk practicing hard without having any guarantees of making the starting team. Do you want to participate on the student council? Again, you must first risk running for school office this quarter—even if you lose.

4. When taking positive risks, are you willing to make the effort successful?

Questions, Activities & Exercises

1. Give three examples of positive risks and three examples of negative risks you have seen classmates take in or outside of school. (Please don't use specific names.)

2. Ask two or three people between age 30 and 60 if there are any risks they wish they would have taken in their lives.

3. Research stories of people who took risks and failed, but kept taking risks until they succeeded. One example is Abraham Lincoln and his persistent run for political office.

4. List risks or struggles associated with the following careers:

   • Professional athlete

   • Company president

   • Inventor

   • Police officer

   • Airline pilot

   • Retail store manager

   • Actor

   • Priest, nun, minister

   • Teacher

   • Parent

   • Politician

   • Author or writer

5. Compare the risks these people probably took in order to succeed with the results of not taking risks.

6. Choose to take a small risk this week. For example:

   • Ask for forgiveness

   • Be nice to someone who isn't a close friend

   • Plan a volunteer activity with your student council

   • Practice your favorite sport an extra 15 minutes

   • Do the dishes or a household chore without being asked

   • Tell your parents that you love them

   • Be nice to your siblings

   • Spend an extra hour on your homework this week

   • Ask someone to help you with a school activity

   • Plan a theme week at school for "kindness" and "respect"

   • Volunteer at a charity

   • Donate money to a charity

   • Break up with someone who isn't right for you

   • Tell friends something you like about them

Journal what you learned from taking a risk. How did you or others benefit? Was there any downside? What is the price of taking risks in your life?

About Ellen Marie, M.S.

Ellen is the founder of Youth Support, Inc., a nonprofit organization promoting leadership skills and sexual abstinence. Ellen is known nationally as a youth expert on sexual abstinence issues and has appeared on national talk shows including Ricki Lake, Montel Williams and the Jesse Ventura Show and in numerous newspapers and radio shows. As a dynamic speaker, Ellen has a unique way of touching the hearts of teens with a practical, sincere message yet adds humor and interaction so teens can truly relate to her message. Her presentations help teenagers understand how they benefit from making tough choices.

Ellen's chapter is dedicated to her 16 year old niece Brittney, who was a passenger killed in an alcohol related traffic accident 12/8/98.

Youth Support, Inc.
P.O. Box 22665, Minneapolis, MN 55422
612-52-YOUTH 612-529-6884
Email: youthspt@aol.com

Resolving Conflict

By Bill Cordes

The Three R's
Every Leader Needs to Know

Resolving Conflict

By Bill Cordes

The Three R's
Every Leader Needs to Know

s Jennifer awoke on Monday morning, she thought of all the ways she could get out of going to school that day.

The past weekend had been too much to handle and she knew that facing her friends would be tough. "Why did they do this to me?" she asked. Here's her story.

Mike, Chris, Alicia, and Kim had been my best friends since the sixth grade. I remember the day of our last day of summer vacation before we started high school. We were nervous about entering high school and made a pact that, no matter what, we'd have each other.

At the beginning of my junior year, I started dating Jeff. They all told me Jeff would treat me badly, but they didn't know him the way I did. He was good to me and I enjoyed the time we spent together. Everyone thought Jeff liked to party—because of his older brother's reputation and because he liked to blast his music as he left the parking lot after school. Yeah, Jeff loved his music but wasn't into drugs like some people thought. We always talked about our desire to stay away from drugs. I knew he was clean; he just had a tough time shaking this bad reputation.

On Friday night, we walked into the Pizza Ranch and my friends were there laughing at us. I went up to their table and asked what was so funny. Mike said, "Hey Jeff, did you get any?" I was floored and didn't say anything. As I stood there too shocked to even imagine why Mike would say such a thing, Alicia piped in, "Cut the act, Jen. What's wrong? Too stoned to talk?" I just bolted out of there. I cried and worried all weekend. Now it's Monday morning and I have to face all of them.

Jennifer is experiencing the destructive force that rumors and conflict can play in a teen's life. She is also at a choice point in her ability to lead and manage a difficult life situation. Her actions here could lay the foundation for how she handles conflict the rest of her life.

Conflict is everywhere. How you choose to *manage* it is a reflection of your character and your ability to be a leader. Change the names and scenario, and this could be a situation you find yourself in.

How do you handle conflict? What would you do in a similar situation?

The First R – Resentment

It would be natural to assume that, based on this situation, Jennifer would feel a lot of resentment toward her peers. (In this case, resentment would be a mild term. You could probably come up with other more outrageous terms to express Jennifer's feelings, but for now let's call it resentment.)

When someone does something to you that you believe they should not have done, you would likely feel resentful. This marks the beginning of a potentially negative, self-destructive thought process.

The feeling of resentment on its own is not self-destructive. In fact, it's natural. But it becomes self-destructive when you move into the second and third "Rs"— resistance and revenge. When your expectations fail to be met, you feel upset or resentful about how someone else handled a situation.

Resentment usually strikes at the very core of your being. Sometimes you feel it in your shoulders or your chest. Sometimes it is a very sick feeling in your gut. Pay attention to where and when you feel resentment. From this place, stop yourself from reacting and focus on responding to that feeling. That makes all the difference in your ability to lead.

The challenge—when you find yourself in a situation like Jennifer's and it is not your fault—is remembering this: *Leadership is not about what happens to you but about how you respond to what happens to you.*

The Second R – Resistance

After you feel resentment, you will likely feel resistance. It's at this point the conflict becomes self-destructive. Because you're mad, you give others the "cold shoulder" or the "silent treatment." What happens when people avoid conflict? It gets worse. Avoidance is not a good strategy for handling conflict.

When she's feeling resentful and resistant, it might seem like a good idea for Jennifer to write her friends off and just avoid them. However, she treasures her friendships. She can realize that, by working this out, she will set a healthy pattern in her teen years that will help her the rest of her life.

Sometimes you can get so stuck in resistance you want to give up on close relationships. Some people stay stuck in resistance for years, never wanting to work things out. By doing so, they begin a pattern of bailing out when things get tough.

Why People Stay Stuck in Resistance

Here are four reasons why people stay stuck in resistance. See if any of these sound familiar.

Reason #1: They want to be right.

They know if they went to parties and discussed the situation, they may realize they were wrong. So they keep to themselves and avoid talking about it. That way, they "get to be right" about their opinions. They feel lonely, but they are right.

Reason #2: They want to punish someone.

Sometimes people get so stuck, they want to punish others by shutting off friendships. It is as if to say, "I'll show you for treating me this way." They may feel a desire to forgive later on but, for the time being, the only desire is to punish them, hoping to make them feel the same resentment and pain.

Yet punishing the people in your life will only bring the same back to you. You have probably heard the phrase "what goes around comes around." Keep in mind as it comes back around, it may not come from the same source but from someone totally different.

Reason #3: They don't know what to do.

Many people do not have a good model for how to handle relationships so the thought of handling the situation in a constructive manner is just not the way to do things. Remember, even though you don't know what to do, you are still responsible for your actions. "I don't know" is simply an excuse that people with bad relationships use to make themselves feel better. Leadership is finding out what to do and improving the quality of your relationships.

Reason #4: They need more time.

This is the only acceptable reason to avoid communication, but there is a catch. You need to let the parties involved know you feel resentful and have a desire to work it out. Keep in mind this is not an easy step in the process of managing conflict, but it is a necessary step. If Jennifer decides she does not want to talk about this today, then it is her responsibility to go to them and speak from her heart about how she feels. Without being harsh, the dialogue would sound something like this: "I am hurt by what was said on Friday night and I want to work this out because our relationship is important to me. I hope that you will give me some time to sort this out and maybe we could discuss it later."

This approach is not easy but, remember, leadership isn't easy either. However, by doing this, Jennifer will put her friends in the right state of mind to discuss the situation. During their time apart, the others will see that you value your friendship and will lay the ground-work for working out the conflict.

The Third R - Revenge

If you stay stuck in the second "R" for long enough, you will eventually move to the third and most destructive "R". Revenge. Does revenge feel good? Sure it does! For a moment. But *only* in the moment. You have heard the saying "if it feels good, do it." That saying should really be "if it feels good tomorrow, do it today."

Though revenge can feel good in the short term, it feels awful after the initial rush of "getting even" wears off. Some people live by the motto "I don't get mad, I get even." The problem with that is we never really get even because if I get even with you, then what do you want to do to me? Get even. Who wins this game? Nobody wins! After enough "getting even," we find ourselves in a no-win situation, the relationship is destroyed and you are destined to go repeat "The Three Rs" in later relationships. You have not learned to manage conflict.

Many people with poor relationships use the self-destructive thought process called the three Rs to handle conflict. Without even thinking, they move through the three Rs, believing this is the way the world works. But living in the three Rs becomes a form of cancer—an energy source that exists within a larger energy source. A cancer eats away at the larger energy source and eventually destroys itself.

When you feel Resentment and Resistance then move into Revenge, you *become* that cancer. You seek to destroy all the people in your life and eventually destroy yourself. If you choose not to work out your conflicts, you expend massive amounts of energy resisting all of the people who could bring joy and happiness. You never experience the joys of leadership, the value of true friendships and enjoyment of living a respectful, joyful, loving life.

You have choice. You are not destined to allow this enemy to run its course every time you feel resentment.

The Solution—OTFDN: Open The Front Door Now

The solution to The Three Rs is like all elements of leadership—simple but not easy. It lies in learning to communicate when conflict comes into your life.

Specifically, learn to communicate by using a process called Open The Front Door Now, or OTFDN. This takes you through a communication process that will support you in handling any conflict. The process is:

O- Share your **Observations** about the situation.

T- Share your **Thoughts** about the situation.

F- Share your **Feelings** about what happened.

D- Share your **Desire** to work this out and improve the relationship.

N- Talk about what you will do the **Next** time a situation like this occurs.

Jennifer can resolve her situation buy using OTFDN, either one-on-one or in a group. She can use her leadership skills to get the parties involved together and speak from her heart. It is important to keep in mind that *how* Jennifer approaches the situation is much more important than *what* she says. She wants to avoid getting bogged down in memorizing a speech or needing to say everything just right. Rather, Jennifer needs to be careful not to blame or put others on the defensive. Most importantly, she communicates from her heart.

Resolving the Conflict

A dialogue Jennifer might use to resolve the conflict goes like this:

Last Friday, I noticed (Observation) you said some things that hurt my feelings. My thoughts (Thoughts) about this are that I was treated unfairly. As a result, I feel (Feel) hurt and resentful. I want (Desire) to talk about this with you and let you know the truth. Most of all, I want (Desire) you to know I care about all of you and I want to be friends. The next time (Next) any of you have anything you would like to say to me, please come to me so we can discuss it directly.

Remember that simply by saying something like this, your responsibilities aren't over. Continue the discussion and the learning for some time. Keep in mind that the parties involved will have a lot to say and the situation may get emotional. Keep speaking from your heart and use only "I" statements. Using statements like "you made me," and "it's your fault" and "you should've done _____" will only send them into experiencing The Three Rs.

Instead, limit your statements to "I feel" and "I want." For example, "I feel upset because of all that has been said and I want to understand how you feel." Keep speaking from your heart and give others plenty of room to make mistakes.

What if you do everything right and still don't get what you want? As you go through life, conflicts will occur and you will not always get what you want. In fact, giving you this OFTDN tool so you could get everything you want would be teaching you how to manipulate people. Manipulation is not the purpose of the tool—it is to keep you out of The Three Rs.

Once you have shared your feelings and discover you do not have a desire to get even with others, you have done all that you can do. Hopefully you will have worked everything out, but sometimes controlling every aspect of the situation isn't possible. It is best just to forgive and move on.

Forgiveness is a tough issue because it comes with an underlying belief that if you forgive others, they will never have to "pay." Remember, you are not forgiving them for *their* sake. You are forgiving them so *you* don't have to go through your life living in the heaviness of The Three Rs.

Forgiveness opens the door to healthy relationships. When you forgive, you drop the negative baggage of relationships that have gone sour. You become a leader.

Questions, Activities & Exercises

Activity #1: A free writing experience
Part 1

This activity is a free writing experience that addresses times in your life when you have had to deal with conflict. With a pen and paper in hand, take five minutes and start writing about conflicts you have experienced. There are no rules; simply list as many situations as possible. Think about conflicts with your parents, times you felt resentful toward your peers, siblings, teachers…even strangers. Write about the situation itself, then how you felt during the situation.

Part 2

Now look at your list and select one of the situations. Write out a dialogue using the strategy for dealing with conflict incorporating the concept of **OFTDN**. If you are not sure how to do this, use the following example as a guide.

Example: I noticed *(observation)* that you did not show up for the study group last night. We really missed you and I was concerned *(thoughts)* about where you were because you did not call. I feel *(feelings)* disappointed because we were really counting on your input and I want *(desire)* you to know that you were missed. I hope the next time *(next)* we schedule a study group, we can count on you to communicate with us if you can't make it.

Activity #2: Understanding the Three Rs

The first stage of the Three Rs is **R** _____ and is usually characterized by a negative feeling toward someone else. When people feel this way, they tend to avoid communication. This stage is called **R** _____ . The only acceptable reason to not communicate with the person we are in conflict with is because we need more _____ . The only catch is that we must let them know that we want to eventually work out the conflict with them. If we don't work out the conflict, we will probably move into the final self-destructive stage called **R** _____ . This stage usually feels good in the moment but destroys others while destroying ourselves in the process.

Activity #3: Unfinished Statements

On a separate sheet of paper, finish the following statements with the first thought that comes to mind. Knowing your answers to these statements will help you identify how you respond to conflict internally so you will not go into the Three Rs.

My inner voice when I am in conflict with someone else usually says…

The area of my body that feels pain when someone hurts me is…

I feel it is necessary to get back at others when they wrong me because…

A resourceful person would handle conflict by…

My automatic response when someone hurts my feelings is to …

A statement I have used in the past that has made the conflict worse is…

The next time I feel hurt instead of avoiding the conflict or trying to get even…

I sometimes choose to avoid conflict because…

A time when I handled a conflict in a positive manner was when…

Positive leaders handle conflicts by listening to others and…

Activity #4: What would you do?

You are walking down the hall at school minding your own business and a friend who you have not spoken to in a few days runs into you. He almost knocks you down. He then looks at you and says, "Hey, watch where you are going, stupid!" Before you can say anything, he walks away laughing.

Before learning about the Three Rs, you would have handled the situation by…

Now that you know about the Three Rs as a resourceful way of handling conflict, you would…(here, write the dialogue and attitude you would use in approaching a conflict.)

Activity #5: Discussion Session

Ask a teacher if you can use this chapter as a forum for discussion about how to handle conflict in school. Start by reading the chapter to the point about using

OTFDN as a tool for handling conflict. Then break the class into groups and discuss how they would handle a similar situation. Have them share their answers with others in the group. Then share the tool **OTFDN** and instruct the members of the class to break into small groups and discuss the question:

Do you think this tool would work in resolving the conflict? Make sure they give reasons why they think it would work. If they don't believe it would work, make sure they give reasons why and offer their own solutions how to handle this conflict in a positive way.

About Bill Cordes

In high school, Bill was voted most likely to be non-academic. He graduated in the Top 10 of the bottom 20% of his class and spent 7.5 years on his undergraduate degree. After a while, Cordes, discovered that many of us struggle with academics and only a few get an education. Since then, he's taught America's youth, college students, and corporate professionals the importance of learning to learn, and "how not to miss life's great opportunities." Bill holds a well-earned Bachelors Degree as well as a Masters Degree in communication. He is a seasoned speaker, teacher and consultant.

Cordes Keynotes and Seminars
2920 Quivera, Great Bend, KS 67530
316-793-7227   fax 316-793-5024   Toll Free: 800-401-6670
Email: YOGOWYPI@aol.com • Web Site: www.BillCordes.com

chapter 15

Overcoming Adversity

By Mike Patrick

Don't Let Anyone Tell You, "You Can't!"

LEAD NOW
or Step Aside!

Overcoming Adversity

By Mike Patrick

Don't Let Anyone Tell You, "You Can't!"

Young or old, teen or adult, we all have problems to face. Stop for a moment and look inside. What are some problems you've had to overcome or are struggling with right now? Drug use? Your best friend moved away? A death or serious illness in the family? Bad grades? Acne? Pressure to be sexual? Divorced parents? Being new to your school? Cut from the team?

Yes, we all struggle with adversity and work to overcome it. I'll begin by telling you one thing that, over the years, I've found to be true. The problem isn't the issue. The issue is how you deal with the problem. Before I explain what I mean by this, here's a concept I really hope you can take to heart. Don't ever let anyone tell you that you can't accomplish something; never underestimate your own capabilities.

Why shouldn't you underestimate yourself? The answer relates to the premise stated above—the problem isn't the issue. The issue is how you deal with the problem.

When a problem occurs, or when you're confronted with a situation that seems hopeless, your attitude

219

determines how you deal with the problem. If you underestimate your abilities, if you say to yourself, "No, there's no way I can deal with this problem or overcome it," you'll be right. If you think you can't, you can't. You probably won't even try. Even if you do try, your attempt will be only half-hearted and you'll give up soon. With the right (positive!) attitude, however, you can overcome all kinds of challenges. If you run into something you can't overcome—a true limitation—at least you can be satisfied you tried your best.

Let's face it, we all have limitations of some sort. Maybe you have diabetes or a learning disability, or maybe you're just nearsighted. Whatever your limitation is, you can learn to deal with it. That's a valuable skill, whether you're a teenager or an adult. Sometimes coming to grips with your limitations can hurt. That's the way it is. We all know that life isn't always easy or fair.

This is a good time to figure out what your strengths and your weaknesses are. Stop now and think about your strengths. What are you good at? Are you honest? A good friend? Kind? Persistent? It's important to know your strengths so you can use them when you have a problem to solve. It's also a good idea to be aware of your weaknesses. Why? Knowing what they are gives you a chance to work on them and eventually build them into strengths.

We don't know what we've got until it's gone.

At this point, you're probably thinking, "How does this Mike Patrick guy know this stuff is true? What makes him an expert on adversity anyway?"

If you could see me, you'd realize why in a second. Since you can't, however, let's go back to a particular day in my life—Friday, September 3, 1971, when I was a high school junior in Worthington, Minnesota. I was class vice president, a member of the National Honor Society and the student council. I was a 16-year-old student/athlete who loved to play football, basketball, baseball, track, golf, and tennis. You name it—if it could be done with a ball, I did it.

That Friday night, I was playing free safety for my school's football team—my very first game for the varsity squad. The opposing team had a reputation for mowing over opponents with a powerful running game, and we *were* getting run over! Near the end of the first half, after one of my teammates sprained his ankle, our coach looked to the bench and waved me into the game.

On my second play, on second-and-goal from the three-yard line, the other team's 205-pound, all-state fullback took the ball and crashed into the center of the line. I hurled my 155-pound body into the gap to stop him. My face mask caught on his kneepad and forced my chin into my neck. When everyone unpiled, I was in terrible pain and, more frighteningly, I couldn't move. Besides the searing pain in my head, I was aware of one other sensation: a tingling feeling that was moving from my chest to my toes. The fifth and sixth vertebrae in my neck respectively were crushed and dislocated, badly damaging my spinal cord. In that brief moment, I broke my neck, became a quadriplegic, and have not walked since.

After I had my accident, my life was extremely difficult for a time. At first, I denied my situation, telling myself and others, "I'm going to be fine. I'm going to walk out of the hospital in a few weeks." When I realized that wasn't going to happen, I felt even more angry and depressed. I didn't like the way I looked or felt. I didn't like myself. I didn't think I had any future. To me, this was as bad as life could get. If I could have killed myself, I would have. But I couldn't even do that!

Don't minimize your problems by comparing them with mine.

Right now you might be thinking, "Wow, being paralyzed—that's a *really* huge problem. The stuff I worry about, well that doesn't amount to anything compared with Mike's challenges."

Please, don't think like that. Though the adversity I have had to overcome has been monumental, don't minimize your problems by comparing them with mine—or with anyone else's. Perhaps when you've talked about a problem with a friend, parent, or teacher, you've been told, "Don't worry, it's really no big deal." Well, if something is going on in your life that feels like a problem, it *is* a problem. Yes, looking back on it a few weeks, months, or years later, you might decide it really wasn't such a big deal. But this isn't the future. It's now. And now, it's a problem!

Ever since my accident, family members, friends and caregivers had been telling me not to worry, that people wouldn't notice my wheelchair, that they would see *me*. Others would see me for what's in my head and heart. "Well, what do you know?" I thought with skepticism. "You're not in my place! You don't have a clue about what I'm going through." Yes, I "knew" all anyone saw was my wheelchair.

During the spring of what would have been my senior year in high school, I enrolled at the local community college. That just wasn't working, so I decided to do something else ... something quite drastic! I had my bags packed for me, flew to San Francisco, and enrolled at the University of California at Berkeley where they had a program for students with disabilities. I told everyone at the time I wanted to live in a warmer climate. But now I realize I was just trying to run away from my situation.

During my second year in California, however, something happened that again changed my life dramatically. That change began two weeks after I had my chair modified. I was leaving the cafeteria with several friends when I zoomed ahead of them to get to the door. I wanted to show them how the modifications had made my chair move much faster.

My friend Karen said, "Whoa, Mike, I didn't know your chair was that fast!" I told her that I recently had it modified, and then asked, "Didn't you notice all the changes in the chair?" She stopped, looked at it carefully, and said, "Oh. Yeah. I guess it *is* different. But you know, Mike, I don't ever really notice the chair, I look at you." My other friends there had exactly the same response.

When I realized people saw "me" not my chair, my attitude changed.

That comment knocked me over. I realized for the first time that people *were* paying attention to me, not to my chair. On that day, my attitude about myself started to change. I began to like who I was again. I began to believe in myself again. And I began to take positive steps in my life. Until I changed how I saw myself, until I decided to have a *positive*—rather than a negative—attitude about myself and my life, I was trapped.

I've had years of adversity to overcome, as you can surely imagine, and I've also had years of successful problem-solving experience. Besides having a positive attitude, it's also important to use a proven process to overcome adversity that I'm about to explain.

Four keys to overcoming adversity

I believe there are four primary keys to overcoming adversity: desire, motivation, persistence, and flexibility. Obviously, these aren't the only factors that determine whether one will succeed, but without them success is unlikely.

Before we look at how these factors affect success, I want to remind you again—*never underestimate your capabilities.* Here's why. While I was still in the hospital after my injury, one of my doctors told me I would never drive a car, never own a home, never sit straight in a wheelchair, never work, or never get married. A rather grim prognosis, don't you think?

Fortunately, I didn't believe him. As a result, I'm now on my fifth van and have driven nearly one-half million miles. I bought my first house when I was 23 and still live in my own home. I can sit straight in my chair; I just need to use a back brace because I also have a broken back. I have created a successful public speaking business. Reaching these goals took time and much effort, but it all started with the belief that I *could* accomplish them.

Key #1: Desire

To overcome adversity, you need to have the desire to solve the problem. This may seem rather obvious, but think about it. If you don't want to do something, it ain't going to happen!

Key #2: Motivation

Once you have the desire to accomplish a task, you need the drive, the incentive, the *motivation* to do so. Take my learning to drive as an example. As I got older, I realized being able to drive would not only give me a great deal of freedom and mobility, it would also open up many opportunities. I once tried to drive a car with hand controls, but found it impossible. Fortunately, the driver training instructor with whom I worked had a positive attitude. "Perhaps with the right equipment, Mike, you *could* drive," he told me. That gave me the desire and the motivation to work harder to solve this problem. This leads to the next key to success.

Key #3: Persistence

Solving a problem requires persistence. You have to keep working at it. Don't give up at the first sign of failure— or the second, or third, or fourth, or fifth. Be persistent. It took me some time to find a company who could design a van with controls that could be adapted to my needs and abilities. Even after I had the van, it needed to have more adjustments made before everything worked correctly. Persistence leads to the fourth key.

Key #4: Flexibility

There is no point in being persistent if you're just going to repeat the first approach you came up with again and again. If Plan A doesn't work, try Plan B. If that doesn't work, go to Plan C. Take different approaches to your problem. Keep trying until you succeed.

A good strategy is to divide a problem into smaller pieces and work on each separately. Let's say, for example, you moved to a new school district and don't know anyone. You feel left out and lonely, and you'd like to have lots of friends. How can you accomplish this?

It's unlikely you could make 10 or 15 new friends in a short time, but you could make one. So you might begin by setting a goal to find one person in the next week who you could eat lunch with. Then the next week, find another. As you get to know one or two people, through them you'll meet more. Eventually, you'll have a new group of friends.

When I broke my neck, the challenge of living with my disability seemed hopeless. Everything that was important to me had suddenly been taken away. Everything I liked to do I did with my arms and legs, but I couldn't move them anymore. My problems felt insurmountable. Eventually, however, my attitude changed and I was able, one step at a time, to begin creating a new life for myself.

We don't know what we've been missing until it arrives.

Focus on flexibility, the last key to success. Being flexible means being open to new ideas and unforeseen solutions. Sometimes a solution is right at hand, but you may not recognize it…or if you do, you may not want to accept it.

When I first tried to drive and failed, I thought I'd never drive again because I was only thinking about driving a regular car. It hadn't occurred to me someone could adapt a car or van to meet my needs—until my driver training instructor mentioned this possibility.

Sometimes when the solution arrives, you'll have to change your perception and be willing to say, "Oh, *that's* the direction I need to go." I tried a number of different jobs before settling into public speaking, and I actually tried a number of speaking jobs before settling into what I now do. I had the desire to work. I had the motivation to look for work. I had the persistence to keep looking and experimenting. I had the flexibility to try different positions until I found something that fit for me. Had I listened to that doctor, I might never have tried to work at all—or I might have tried only one or two jobs and then given up when they didn't work out. I love my work today, but I didn't know what I'd been missing until it arrived.

Here's still another example of how attitude and outlook is so important to eventual success in overcoming adversity. I could have seen my various "failed" attempts at working as just that—failures. What is called "failure" may not, however, be failure. Think of "failures" as markers pointing you in a new direction.

Eventually you will reach a solution, and when you do, you'll realize that, without your "failures," you might never have found it. When dealing with adversity, be flexible. Be persistent. Open your mind to as many possibilities as you can. Be creative.

Remember, as Henry Ford once said, "Whether you think you can or whether you think you can't—*you're right!*"

Questions, Activities & Exercises

Below are four fun and insightful group activities for helping leaders learn to overcome adversity. Try them one at a time, then follow each activity by discussing the sample discussion questions with all participants:

1. Finding a Group's Birth Date Order

Begin by telling the group their task is to line up by birth date order—not by year, just birth date—from January 1st to December 31st. But wait! There's a catch! Tell them they can't talk to each other or to you while they're trying to accomplish this task.

Facilitator tips:

Urge the group to be flexible and creative. There are many ways, besides speaking, we can communicate. Anything goes—sign language, showing driver's licenses, writing and so on—as long as they aren't talking. Tell them, "If one technique doesn't work, try something else. Be creative." But do not give them any ideas about alternative methods of communication!

2. How Many Ducks Are Needed?

Tell the group they have to solve the problem you're about to describe. Then read the following:

> *You have two ducks behind a duck. You have two ducks in front of a duck. You have one duck in the middle. What is the lowest number of ducks you need to fit these three statements?*

Facilitator tips:

Participants often say five ducks are needed, but, of course, the correct answer is three. Point out in the discussion it's important to break down problems into smaller pieces so they don't seem overwhelming. Doing so also enables people to have smaller more immediate successes as they try to solve the larger problem—which provides encouragement and the reinforcement to continue working. In this particular case, you actually have three separate problems.

3. Touchless Huddle

Choose an object like a school backpack or something of similar size. Tell group members their task is to figure out a way for all of them to touch the object at the same time, but *without* touching one another. After they accomplish this task, have them repeat the exercise, but with a smaller object—a paper cup, for example. Next, repeat the exercise once more but reduce the size of the object even further—use a quarter or a pencil for example. Each group should have between 8 and 15 participants.

4. Blind Trust Walk

Divide your group into pairs, preferably pairing each with someone they don't know (or at least someone who's not a good friend). Each pair can be male/female or the same gender. Tell the partners to choose who will be non-sighted first. Then the "sighted" persons guide their "blind" partners on a five-to-ten-minute walk. Explain that this "relationship" requires great trust, since they are not allowed to touch one another during the walk. Remind them of the following sayings and ask them to think about how these sayings might apply to this exercise: "Two wrongs don't make a right." "What goes around, comes around." "Revenge is sweet."

Sample discussion questions for each exercise:

- Did you apply the four keys to this problem? Give examples.

- What problems did you encounter in trying to solve this problem?

- What feelings and thoughts did you have while trying to solve the problems you encountered? Fear? Frustration? "It's impossible!" Excitement? Wanting to give up? What did you do with those feelings and thoughts?

- Why is it important to listen carefully to directions?

- How many ways did you find to communicate with one another as a group?

- Did any one person come up with all the solutions? If not, what does that tell you about the benefits of seeking help and cooperating when you have a problem to overcome?

About Mike Patrick

Mike got the electric chair and lived to tell about it—the electric wheelchair, that is. Mike is a motivational speaker and health educator with good news to tell. The good news is, we are all very capable people. We all need to recognize those capabilities and then learn to use them. Mike helps you do just that with candor, wit and humor. What he has to say will make you laugh. Some of it will make you cry. He will guarantee you this, it will make you "Think About It."

Patrick Communications, Inc.

3225 Emerson Avenue South, Minneapolis, MN 55408-3523
612-827-4110   fax 612-824-9229   Toll Free: 800-972-9537
E-mail: mike@patcom.com • Web Site: www.patcom.com

chapter 16

Managing Stress

By Susie Vanderlip

From Stress Cadet to Successful Leader

LEAD NOW
or Step Aside!

Managing Stress

By Susie Vanderlip

From Stress Cadet to Successful Leader

L eadership can add a lot of pressure, especially when your life also includes athletics, theater, choral groups, service clubs, homework, SATs, college applications, exams, term papers, a job, and your parents' expectations. How you handle it determines your success with respect to your ability to lead others.

Consider the following questions:

- When you put your head on the pillow at night, is your mind filled with thoughts, plans, and details that will help you control the next day?

- Do you rethink conversations you had today, analyzing what you should have said or what you will say to "make things right" or "get even" tomorrow?

- Have you ever put in lots of time and energy on an event for school, and when it was over, felt totally exhausted, depressed, JOYLESS?

Does any of the above ring a bell? Then read on, fellow "stress cadet!"

Stress Can Be Positive

Some stress works to motivate people in a necessary, even healthy way.

Would you ever complete a paper if you didn't have a due date? Given a choice, most people would rather spend time in a chat room, on an athletic field, or hanging with friends. Yet deadlines create a positive stress that helps you get things accomplished.

Dangers of Too Much Stress

Too much stress, on the other hand, makes people cranky, unhappy, and even ill. Whether it's mental, emotional, or physical, too much stress can lead to poor health, mental illness, a dismal outlook, and lowered productivity.

Excess stress can have a serious impact on leaders. Ever have a leader who bosses everyone else around, doesn't delegate tasks to others, acts as though he or she is the only one who can do things right? Leaders who won't release control may actually be out-of-control due to stress. Leaders who do not manage their stress can create an unhappy team. Motivation, cooperation, and team spirit drop when a leader becomes pushy, irritable, ill-tempered. A team under too much pressure may become gossipy, and gossip damages trust, team spirit, and morale. Therefore, leaders actually have a responsibility to those they lead to relax and reduce their stress.

Some leaders fall prey to the common misconception that they can eliminate stress by smoking cigarettes, drinking, or doing drugs. These choices only cover up anxiety and suppress feelings. Once the "high" wears off, worry, frustration, anxiety, and overwhelm almost always return and often to a greater degree because the cause was never dealt with.

Effects of Too Much Stress

Stress can cause many physical problems like stomachaches, headaches, migraines, asthma attacks, a pounding heart, fast breathing, trembling, nervous tics, teeth grinding, even bedwetting. One teen under stress may not be able to fall asleep while another may not be able to wake up. Some teens overeat to obesity due to stress, while others undereat and develop anorexia or bulimia.

Mental problems like forgetfulness, accident-proneness, anxiety, insecurity, and fear can occur. Many teens worry about what other people think of them, and may isolate from others to avoid discomfort or feeling out of place. Isolation, however, can cause severe loneliness that, in itself, is very stressful.

Too much stress can make us fragile and feel like crying over the smallest things. Some people react to pressure with anger and rage, lashing out with violence. Even high-achievers can find themselves thinking suicidal thoughts under excessive stress because they assume they have to be perfect to be liked or want to please their parents.

Stress can affect us on a spiritual level as well, robbing us of joy in our lives. Without some joy, it is easy to feel unwanted, unloved, and alone. Many faiths speak of deep loneliness as a separation from God. *Too much stress can bury us in fear rather than uplift us in faith.*

Common Sources of Stress

- Situations at home
  (e.g., parents fighting, criticizing or violence; abuse of alcohol or drugs in the family; verbal, physical, or sexual abuse)

- Parents' separation or divorce
- New step-parent
- New school
- Death of a loved one
- New sister or brother
- Single-parent household
  (e.g., lack of money; carrying "adult" responsibilities like cooking, raising younger siblings, hearing a parent sharing adult matters that teens would rather not know about)
- Personal stresses
  (e.g., grades; homework; leadership responsibilities; breakup with a boy/girl friend; competition like sports, performing arts, college applications; pressure to be popular, to use or not use drugs, to have sex or abstain; sexual consequences like pregnancy, STDs, AIDS)

How to Handle Stress in a Positive Way

The first step is to identify when stress has become too much for YOU because everybody reacts differently.

TAKE YOUR STRESS TEMPERATURE

Rate your stress level throughout the day. Make a note in your day planner using a scale of 1 to 5.

  1 - I feel relaxed.

  2 - I'm busy, motivated, and excited about life.

  3 - I've got too much to do; I am showing signs of stress.

  4 - I AM *VERY* STRESSED! I have clear signs of too much: physically, emotionally, mentally or spiritually ill, bummed, depressed, anxious, worried.

5 - TAKE ME TO THE PSYCH WARD! I am DANGEROUS to myself or others (having suicidal thoughts; wanting to hurt self or others; isolating, using drugs, alcohol, or sex to cope)

- Keep track for one whole week. Notice when you show signs of too much stress. Jot down what day and time, where you are, what classes you are in, and which people you are around.

- Then list steps that might help with the people, places, and things that are stressing you out.

- Talk over the list with a friend or counselor. Some of the ideas you'll keep; some you'll throw out.

- PRIORITIZE your solutions. Take them one at a time. Try to complete a task before you go on to the next one.

- At the end of the day, remind yourself, "I did exactly as much as I was supposed to today."

- As you put your head on the pillow, think of five things you did right today.

- Then get a good night's sleep and tackle what's next on your list tomorrow.

Release Stress from Your Body

Start by giving the body what it needs most—oxygen. BREATHE!

Most people take shallow breaths into the upper part of their lungs only. Deep breathing is the first step to reducing the stress response in your body. Here are some suggestions:

- Begin by relaxing your shoulders and arms.

- Slowly circle your head to the right, then the left.

- Repeat several times.

- Then take a slow, deep breath. Exhale. Repeat. Let each breath fill your stomach, then your chest, and then feel it lift your shoulders. Take your first breath in to a slow count of 5, then exhale to a slow count of 5. As you exhale, let your shoulders drop, your chest relax, and your stomach muscles pull in.

Your mind may wander, worry, or get annoyed. Just notice your reaction and refocus your attention on the slow, even flow of your breath. Breathing is the first step to releasing stress and making room for positive possibilities.

Yoga for the Classroom

When stress builds around responsibilities or confrontations, find quick relief in YOGA. Yoga is a 5,000-year-old practice of physical stretches with deep breathing. It releases happy hormones (endorphins) and re-energizes the body, mind and spirit. For more information, find a book on Yoga in the library, take a class, or order a full *De-Stress for Success* book.

Do these Yoga side-bends:

- Place feet together in parallel.

- Extend both arms over your head, hands palm to palm.

- Take a deep breath. Inhale, filling your belly, middle chest, and lifting your shoulders.

- Exhale and lean your body to the left, arms still extended along side your head.

- While to the side, slowly inhale and exhale two more times. Imagine you are inhaling into all the uncomfortable places on your right side and neck. As you exhale, relax every muscle on the right.

- On the fourth inhale, rise back to center, then repeat by leaning to your right. Repeat with two more deep inhales and exhales. Breathe into the left side of your body and neck. On the third inhale, rise back to center, let your arms drop gently back to your sides.

Does any area of your body feel warmer, more relaxed, or more open? That's the goal! Energy flow!

Release Stress from Your Mind

Much stress comes from what we think of ourselves and of situations in our lives. Everyone gets caught up in worry, desire, or obsession at some time in life. We do, however, have some power over our thoughts. It begins with how we talk to ourselves.

Every human being does talk to himself or herself. And most have a critical voice within their minds that judges them as stupid, a loser, ugly, or unlovable at times. Psychologists call this "negative self-talk."

We tend to be more productive and enjoy life more when we replace negative self-talk with supportive, caring statements like: *"I don't have to be perfect to be loved."*

If you repeat this statement to yourself five times, slowly and thoughtfully, you can get "off your case" and increase your confidence.

When under stress, we need to feed our brains consistent, positive reminders of our worth: *Life isn't about perfection. It is about "perfecting." It is enough to make a little progress each and every day!*

Another "STRESS BUSTER" for your brain, body, and spirit is The HALT Principle: when you feel

too **Hungry,**
too **Angry,**
too **Lonely,** or
too **Tired** . . .
HALT!!!

Check out your physical well being first, because when you are too hungry or too tired, feelings of anger, worry, excitement, and upset are often intensified or exaggerated. You lose your ability to perceive reality clearly.

Anger and loneliness are two of the most powerful and stressful emotions. If you let yourself get too angry, you become ripe for arguments that can even escalate into violence. Or if you get too lonely and depressed, You may perhaps become suicidal.

Anger

Notice when you begin to feel angry. Don't wait until you are enraged and vengeful. Diffuse anger early by talking it out with a friend, peer helper, conflict manager, counselor, parent, or other adult you trust. No need to feel embarrassed. It is more important that you get support in handling anger and identifying healthy, concrete options for solving problems.

Some teens get angry because they have unrealistic expectations of their friends, family, teachers, or others.

When you are angry at others, ask yourself, "What did I expect? Did I expect them to act the way I would? Did I expect them to act the way *I* wanted them to, not the way they really are?"

When Angie was a high school junior, her friend Lenore always flirted with the guys Angie liked. Angie would get furious. She hated fighting, so she stewed inside, got migraine headaches, sometimes even threw up. She heard about The HALT Principle, so the next time she was angry with Lenore, she talked it out with peer helpers on her campus. With their assistance, she decided to confront Lenore. The next time Lenore flirted with Angie's boyfriend, Angie got up her nerve and said, without yelling or scolding, "I felt uncomfortable when you flirted with my boyfriend. Please stop or I can't continue to be friends with you."

Lenore got mad and walked away. A day later, however, Lenore came back and apologized. She admitted she was feeling left out and afraid of losing Angie's friendship to the boyfriend. Angie and Lenore gained understanding and compassion for each other, scheduled time together, and kept their friendship alive.

Though it is embarrassing to express feelings at times, talking out anger can keep you from exploding at people you truly care about, or from blaming yourself and getting depressed.

Loneliness

Loneliness has the power to push people to extremes, as well. When you feel like you don't fit in or are being treated like you don't belong, walk away from people who are being unkind or inconsiderate. Find a friend, a teacher, a counselor, you can trust. Let them know you need support at that moment. Accept a hug from them.

You don't have the power to make everybody like you! The important thing is that you like yourself enough to ask trustworthy people for the attention and kindness you need and deserve.

Positive Mental Filters

Many teens, including leaders, have a parent or parents who put them down or criticize them. This creates considerable stress. A number of teens drink, smoke dope, and do other drugs just to stop the terrible feelings they have as the result of someone's verbal abuse.

You can help yourself by becoming your own "encourager" as well as encouraging your friends. Reduce the damage and stress of verbal abuse by using the following three "positive mental filters."

1. *JUST BECAUSE THEY SAY IT, DOESN'T MAKE IT SO!*

Shareen's dad drank heavily. When he was drinking, he put her down viciously, saying, "You'll never amount to anything! You're a mistake!" Her dad's words upset her greatly until she learned to use the phrase: *"Just because he says it, doesn't make it so."*

When he was verbally cruel to her, Shareen would repeat this to herself five times. The first time she thought it, she still felt bad. But by the fifth time, she saw it was absurd to believe words out of the mouth of someone who had been drinking. She got the truth; it was alcohol that made him abusive, not her!

2. WHAT OTHER PEOPLE THINK OF ME IS NONE OF MY BUSINESS. WHAT I THINK OF ME IS MY BUSINESS!

Raymond was a high school sophomore born with a deformed foot. All his life, he was called "Gimp!" and "Nerd!" Raymond could have felt like a complete loser, but his mother had told him as a little boy:

> "Raymond, if you think you are what other people call you, then that IS what you will always be. But, if you quietly ask yourself, *What do I think of me right now?* and listen with your heart, you will know that you are special. Remember, *What other people think of you is none of your business; what you think of you is your business.*"

When Raymond got to high school, he remembered his mother's words. Other guys thought Raymond was a fool to go out for football. They did not know Raymond had spent hours learning to control his deformed foot by kicking cans and rocks, and eventually a football. Raymond became the best punter in his league because he didn't let what others thought of him stress him out. He thought of himself as an athlete, not a "gimp" or a "nerd." And an athlete he became!

3. OVERCOME FEAR

One of the biggest stressors in life is FEAR! You can bust "fear" if you recognize what it really is:

False

Expectations

Appearing

Real

No one really knows what the future will bring, not even one minute from now. Worry is merely your imagination creating fearful pictures of the future. Worry does not prevent bad things from happening. It actually gets in the way of finding positive solutions because it paralyzes and limits your thinking.

Ashley was a sophomore who hated 5th period because Cheri was in that class. Cheri threatened to beat Ashley up before 5th period on Monday morning. Ashley was in FEAR. She worried all weekend. She imagined herself in the hospital in a full body cast! By 4th period on Monday, Ashley's stress triggered a serious asthma attack and she was sent home. That evening, a friend called Ashley and shared, "Cheri got caught smoking pot in the bathroom before 5th period and was expelled from school. She won't ever bother you again."

Ashley's worst fear never happened. Unfortunately, by imagining the worst, Ashley's stress ruined her whole weekend, caused her asthma attack, and affected her grade because she missed an exam that afternoon.

Don't give FEAR power. Talk it out with someone. You may choose to pray or meditate, read something spiritual that gives you hope, and entrust the future to a spiritual power/God you believe in. Spiritual leaders of many faiths have said: *"Courage is simply fear that has said its prayers!"*

Make TODAY good to take the best possible care of the FUTURE.

Release Stress from Your Spirit!

If you think of "spirit" as "enthusiasm for life," then too much stress makes people feel unmotivated and hopeless. Combat stress with recreation, reaching out, and putting first things first.

1. PLAY, ENJOY, TAKE UP A HOBBY

Participate in competitive sports and also make time for FUN where no one is a winner or loser. Be creative: sculpt, draw, take photographs, write stories or poetry, play a musical instrument, sing, dance. Celebrate your unique talents and express yourself. Be with nature: watch the stars, walk in the woods, play with your pets, garden, ride the surf.

People often spend time using logic and thinking with the left side of their brains. Creative fun taps into the right side of the brain, encouraging new dreams, ideas, and insights.

2. REACH OUT TO OTHERS FOR SUPPORT

My high school boyfriend, who later became my husband, refused to talk about his feelings, especially the emotions of hurt, fear, anger, and worry. He would demand to be left alone. As time went on, he drank, smoked dope, and took pills to deal with stress, but his stress never went away permanently. The alcohol and drugs only masked his feelings.

As his stress increased, he used more alcohol and drugs to escape his feelings and isolated more from the people who cared about him, even from me. He became addicted. He lost his ability to think wisely. Common to those who are addicted, he angrily refused to talk about his problems or seek help. At long last and quite sadly, he lost his life to an unintentional overdose of alcohol, cocaine, and prescription drugs—alone and isolated.

Play it safe. Play it smart. Reach out and ask for support to deal with stress.

3. PUT FIRST THINGS FIRST

I once had a boss who was paraplegic and used a wheelchair. When he felt stressed or scared, he couldn't just run away. When we had deadlines breathing down our necks, he would wisely say to me: "Save your panic until you really need it." What he meant was, "Don't stress out unless it is truly necessary. Don't sweat the small stuff!"

During times of fear and anxiety, ask yourself, "How important is it?" Is this situation really a crisis or just an irritating bump in the road? CHOOSE not to take a minor worry too seriously. And, crisis or not, BREATHE, think H-A-L-T, and remember: *The reason angels can fly is that they don't take themselves too seriously!*

Questions, Activities & Exercises

1. LOOK FOR THE POSITIVE

Take a break during stressful times and organize everyone into pairs. Direct people to think of three things they have done right today, then share the answers in their pairs. The partners should acknowledge one another by saying, "Good job!"

This process helps them recognize how much more they are doing right than they may be doing wrong, and relieves a lot of pressure.

2. INFUSE A LITTLE HUMOR

Start meetings with different people telling short, clean jokes. Rotate the person who shares so everyone practices his or her sense of humor. Share the laughter.

3. GROUP STRESS REDUCTION

Try a "group scream" to relieve tension. On the count of three, everyone yells at the top of their lungs in unison. Give three rounds of earth-shattering yells to relieve the stress, energize the crowd, and generate a few laughs.

4. GROUP STRETCH WITH SHOULDER RUBS

Lead the group through the Yoga stretches with deep breathing (and group groans!). Afterwards, have everyone face clockwise in a circle and for two minutes, rub the neck and shoulders of the person in front. Reverse the direction of the circle and rub again. This combo combats stress and builds camaraderie, and is especially good before a big group event.

5. HELP YOURSELF AND OTHERS KEEP A BRIGHT ATTITUDE

Pay attention to the small things that make you feel good. Having someone listen and encourage you helps you maintain a positive attitude.

Pair people up. Have them listen to each other's concerns without interrupting or judging. Offer positive suggestions to each other and avoid saying "You

SHOULD" or "You HAVE TO." Try starting your sentences with "I SUGGEST you…" This allows listeners to evaluate the idea for themselves without feeling stupid or feeling like a failure. They can come to their own conclusions without feeling like they have to agree with or please you. This reduces stress in making personal decisions.

Stress is a state of mind. As a remarkable speaker and colleague of mine W. Mitchell always says: *"It's not what happens to you, it's what you do about it."*

About Susie Vanderlip

Susie partners with schools and communities committed to guiding teens successfully through the landmines of adolescence including alcohol and drugs, teen violence, sexuality, gangs, suicide, and the handicap of emotional distress. She is an extraordinary speaker! Using talents as a professional actress, Hip Hop and Jazz dancer, prevention specialist and Certified Speaking Professional, Susie delivers a captivating theatrical program, *LEGACY OF HOPE'*. She shares life-saving conversations with teens from troubled homes, and trains at-risk to leadership teens in coping with stress/emotional upset in *DE-STRESS FOR SUCCESS'*. Her web site links to RESOURCES OF HOPE for both teens and families. Contributing-author in *Teen Power Too*.

Legacy
4642 E. Chapman Ave., Suite 112, Orange, CA 92869
714-997-2158   fax 714-997-0401   Toll Free: 800-707-1977
Email:BookSusie@legacyofhope.com • Web Site: www.legacyofhope.com

chapter 17

Raising the Roof!

Awesome Ideas for Raising Money, Spirit, and Awareness

LEAD NOW
or Step Aside!

Raising the Roof!

Awesome Ideas for Raising Money, Spirit, and Awareness

Each of the ideas in this chapter have been submitted by one of *Lead Now's* sixteen co-authors. Our cumulative experience in working with thousands of schools and leadership groups has left us with a lot of really cool ideas that work!

We've racked our brains to compile the "best of the best" and are sharing with you proven ways to make a positive impact in your school or organization. There are no right or wrong ways to execute these activities and projects. If you see one you want to try, feel free to change or alter it to fit your unique situation.

It is important to note that not all ideas will work for all groups. You may see some activities below that would not be approved by your school's administrators or your organization's sponsors. This is why it is imperative to always get approval and/or permission from necessary authorities before planning any type of activity. That said, let's "raise the roof!"

Awesome Ideas for Raising Money

Swap Meet *submitted by Eric Chester*

Every home in your community is filled with stuff the owners no longer want but can't throw away. Setting up garage sales is a hassle, so arrange a swap meet (flea market) in your school's parking lot! Give yourself plenty of lead time to promote it, then schedule a Saturday when community residents can buy a parking space and "set up shop" to sell their stuff. If you sell 200 parking spaces for $15 each, you just made a cool $3,000 in a day. And if you promote it well enough, you can charge admission to the buyers at 50 cents each. Then multiply your profits by setting up concessions with hot dogs, popcorn, soda, etc. The possibilities are endless!

Dash for Cash *submitted by Phil Boyte*

This is similar to a 50-50 raffle. During a basketball game, you collect dollars from people who want a chance to dash for cash. You give each person a ticket and put the matching ticket into a can. This can holds all the tickets you will draw from later. At the game's half-time break, you take half of the money collected and put it away for your profit. Lay out the other half of the money on the basketball court. Spread the one-dollar bills about three feet apart to make it more of a challenge. Draw a winning ticket from the can and that ticket holder will get 30 seconds to dash onto the court and collect as many one-dollar bills as possible. As an example, one school collected $200 in donations, then set $100 on the floor. In 30 seconds, the "dasher" collected $34 dollars and the remaining $64 became additional profit for the school.

Team Talent Show and Silent Auction *submitted by Tony Schiller*

Promote a school-wide talent show in which all the acts will be performed by various organized clubs and sports teams throughout your school. Limit skits and acts to eight minutes or less. Establish a rule that says teams *cannot* perform acts that contain skills from their specific area of talent (i.e., the "school band" team must do something other than play instruments, the "basketball players" team cannot spin balls, etc). Judges will evaluate teams on talent, creativity, costumes/staging, and school spirit. (Perhaps you can secure local celebrity judges!) The admission price should be low enough to fill your auditorium. Now for the key to the real fund raising within this activity—a silent auction! Before the show, hold a silent auction with several items donated by local businesses up for bid. Invite the participating "talent teams" to secure donations by allowing each team to keep 50% of the money bid from those specific items. Announce winning bids immediately after the show. Elements for success to this event include high attendance, quality donations for the auction, and a well-produced talent show.

Halloween Insurance Policies *submitted by Kevin Wanzer*

Sell insurance policies to neighbors to insure them against anything that may happen to their home as a result of Halloween pranks. If their homes are pelted with eggs, covered with toilet paper, or graced with a nice baggy of Doggy Do-Do on a front porch, neighbors need not fret. They simply call your Ghostbusters patrol and, in a jiffy, your team members will arrive to clean up the scene. People really do buy these policies!

Couch Potato *submitted by Craig Hillier*

In this idea, a lucky winner in a drawing gets to watch a game, a special activity, or a pep rally from the best seat in the house. Here's how it works: Locate a comfortable couch (the owner of a furniture store might donate one if the store is given enough recognition). Depending on the event, the couch should be positioned on the sidelines or in the stands. (Some schools actually have a platform specially built for the couch.) Students then sell tickets prior to the game or event, usually at 50 cents each or three for a dollar. You draw a ticket on the day of the game and the winner and a guest get to sit in the couch for that particular activity. A courtside seat! Some schools even have one couch for students and a separate one for parents. *You might want to "sweeten the pot" by throwing in a $10 shopping spree at the concession stand and have a faculty member serve snacks to the couch potato(es). This is a *pure profit* event because the concession money goes back to the school or booster club.

Faculty Dress Down Day *submitted by Jeff Yalden*

(This only works in schools where the faculty members have a business-attire-only dress code.) Plan a day when teachers can purchase the right to dress down! Each participant who pays $5.00 gets administrative authorization to dress down for that day. One hundred faculty members playing along would equal $500 and a lot of laughs! Kids at these schools don't normally get to see their teachers in jeans and t-shirts. *Some kids will finally see that their teachers are actually real people!*

TEEN POWER Book Sale with a Girl Scout Cookie Twist
submitted by Mike Patrick

Have you ever sold, or bought, Girl Scout Cookies? If the answer is "Yes" then you have experienced pre-selling a product. Your group can raise funds without spending any money upfront by pre-selling the *Teen Power* book series for the full $11.95 price per book. Remember that speaker who came to your school and said s/he was one of the authors of the *Teen Power* book series? Go to the back of the book you bought that day to find the contact information. Call those contacts and ask if they would sell you a large quantity of the four books at a large discount. I'm willing to bet they would! You sell the books, collect the money, send $6.00 a book (or maybe less) to the speaker you're working with, and you've just made $5.95 (or maybe more) a book for your group. Instead of a perishable product made mostly of sugar or salt, you sell a wonderful gift set of books. These worthwhile products are easily shared with others and will last a lifetime.

Coupon Clipping *submitted by Kevin Wanzer*

Have group members collect coupons for various grocery items. On the back of each coupon, write the initials of your school or group. Partner with a local grocery store and school supporter where each week, your group will tape the respective coupons to various products. When people go shopping and see a coupon taped to a product they are interested in, they will more than likely buy that particular item. When the coupon is redeemed at the register, the grocer then tallies the amount of money saved by the various coupons supplied by your group and reimburse your group for that amount of money. In addition, you might have a sign at each cash register explaining your group's mission. It would ask them to donate the money they saved from your coupons to your group. From a dollar coupon, you then make two dollars.

I've Got a Crush on You! *submitted by Byron V. Garrett*

About three weeks before a special day (usually Valentine's day), begin the promotional campaign for *I've Got a Crush on You!* Individuals who have a crush on someone else (or they may just be great friends) will sign up to send them a CRUSH soda on that special day. CRUSH soda comes in two sizes; they can choose to send the 12oz. can for $1.00 or go all-out with the 2-liter bottle for $2.50. Work with a local soft drink distributor to get the CRUSH drinks at a discounted rate. Encourage everyone to send a crush to a friend, teacher, boyfriend/girlfriend, and so on. For effect, individually wrap the can(s) or bottle(s) in white tissue paper or another color and attach a paper heart with ribbon and a message from the admirer. Arrange for a pick-up and delivery station in the commons or school cafeteria. Simply create an alphabetical list of recipients and the number/size of crushes for pickup. This new twist on the "candy-gram" sale is a lot of fun.

Halloween Candy Sales *submitted by Kevin Wanzer*

With your leadership group, go trick or treating on November 1. Ask residents for any leftover candy they have from the night before. (People typically have tons of left over candy they did not give out or have confiscated from their trick-or-treating munchkins.) Collect all the candy and divide it equally into sandwich baggies. Then use that candy as your fund raising items to sell at school. No more commissions. No more selling three candy nuggets for $1.50 a box. This fundraiser is 100% profit and 100% fun!

Awesome Ideas for Raising Spirit

Life is an Adventure Day *submitted by Susie Vanderlip*

Coordinate a campus-wide "Life is an Adventure Day" in which you focus on planning for a career and looking into new hobbies. Contact representatives from a variety of fun and interesting careers and hobbies like scuba diving, sky diving, travel and tourism, internet website designing, fashion modeling, television and radio, auto racing, etc. Invite them to set up booths so students can talk with them to get an idea of all the fun careers and hobbies that exist. Then have a "dream job" contest in which participants demonstrate their "dream job" by using cut out pictures from magazines, drawings, pictures, etc.

Above and Beyond Pep Rally *submitted by Eric Chester*

Surprise your student body by holding a pep rally where athletics is not even mentioned. Instead, honor students who represent the school and demonstrate excellence in activities other than sports. Pay tribute to outstanding members representing activities like band, choir, chess, speech and drama, yearbook/journalism, DECA, FBLA, auto mechanics, etc. Get a local celebrity to introduce each honoree and tell the audience what makes them "above and beyond" the norm. You'll be amazed at the increase in total school spirit when you widen your circle to honor outstanding achievement beyond sports.

Warm Fuzzy Bags *submitted by Susie Vanderlip*

Having an on-campus conference or leadership retreat? Grab brown paper bags, glitter, felt pens, and stickers. Have all participants write their names on bags and decorate them in way hey like. Then tape every bag onto a wall where everybody can get to them. Have pieces of scratch paper and pens around all day so each person can write a "warm fuzzy note" (something encouraging or something nice about the person) to, hopefully, everyone before the event is over. It's GREAT to get a paper bag full of friendship notes and compliments at the end of a retreat or conference.

Kisses for Royalty *submitted by Kevin Wanzer*

To get everyone involved in Homecoming or Prom activities, pass out blank, white index cards to each student two weeks before the dance. Give each student the opportunity to take the cards, put on lipstick (in the privacy of his or her own home), and "kiss the card" putting lip imprints on the front of each card. On the back, they neatly write their names in small print. When the cards are returned to school, the lips are divided by sexes and displayed on the walls of the cafeteria the week prior to the dance. The students vote on the best set of lips, with no idea whose lips belong to whom. Once the votes are tallied, those voted as the "best set of lips" are announced as part of the dance's royalty.

Awesome Ideas for Raising Awareness

Post-it Education *submitted by Byron V. Garrett*

During diversity week or multicultural day, gather hundreds of facts in short phrases about specific cultures. Place these facts on post-it notes, posters, and post cards. On Monday, display posters throughout the campus with various multicultural facts. On Tuesday, have the school office mail a diversity post card (again containing facts) to the home of each person on campus. On Thursday, as the momentum picks up, begin placing the post-it notes everywhere—from the back of the bathroom stall doors to cafeteria trays to vending machines. People will notice and remember the messages the see around the campus and especially those that have been sent to their home.

Liquor-less Libations Bar *submitted by Susie Vanderlip*

Promote a dance where only those who sign a contract to remain alcohol and drug-free are admitted. Do it up big! At the dance, have a "Liquor-less Libations Bar" providing yummy alcohol-free drinks. (For a great booklet of recipes contact: California State Automobile Association 415-565-2297.) You'll get a lot of support and even "freebies" by community groups who are committed to your cause. You'll even get a lot of free publicity!

Take A Stand Against Violence *submitted by Karl Anthony*

On the first Monday of every month, call for one minute of silence to reflect on non-violence. Start by gaining attention through a very short reading, poem or song over the intercom. Then follow up with sixty seconds of silence to focus on non-violence, remembering students who have been hurt or killed in schools across America. This activity takes a few short minutes, but the feeling in your school will be amazing when everyone unites to takes a stand for something truly important.

Christmas in July *submitted by Phil Boyte*

Many schools get excited about community service during the holiday season. As a result, people in senior citizens' homes receive a lot of attention all at once. What would happen if you went into an old folks' home and threw a Christmas Party in July? Find an artificial tree and grab ornaments from your garage. Make some Christmas cookies and desserts, and head with your group to the senior home. (Be sure to call first and set a date with the director.) When you get there, set up the party, serve the desserts, and sing carols with the seniors. They will love the attention and time spent with young people. One school group even pooled some money to buy a video game set, then gave it as a gift because they had heard video games help seniors keep their minds active and playful.

Raise Awareness on Campus *submitted by Susie Vanderlip*

If you don't already have a sober and drug free club, create one. Ask your counselor or favorite teacher to be the advisor and get you started. You can have a SADD Club (Students Against Destructive Decisions—national SADD organization at 508-481-3568), or PRIDE (800-853-7867) or Youth to Youth (614-224-4506), Friday Night Live (in California), or make up your own! Consider a project like raising awareness on campus with a speaker and booths for information by calling Alcoholics Anonymous, Al-Anon (for family and friends of problem drinkers), the police department, and local rehab hospitals. Have lots of pamphlets out that you can get for FREE from the National Clearinghouse for Alcohol and Drug Information (NCADI) at 1-800-729-6686 or www.health.org. Survey every student the next day to see who wants peer helpers and support groups on campus. Preventing drunk driving accidents and helping teens cope with suicidal or violent feelings is for everyday, not just Red Ribbon Week.

Mentor at the Middle School *submitted by Susie Vanderlip*

Help middle school kids prepare to come to high school by writing a play about high school. Have all participants keep a journal for a couple of weeks. Then each should create a character dealing with some of the real life challenges of high school. Get permission for your group to visit a nearby middle school and work with 8th graders presenting short skits. Then answer their questions. You can even let the 8th graders role play by assuming parts in the skits to show how they would handle challenges like being gossiped about, or being offered alcohol or drugs. In the fall, when the new 9th graders arrive, assign them an upperclass "mentor" to show them around and help them adjust to life in high school.

Youth Center for Teens with Nothin' to Do!
submitted by Susie Vanderlip

Create a Youth Center in your community. With the help of your advisor, prepare a statement about why you feel there is a need for a Youth Center where teens can hang out (a place that is alcohol and drug-free and has activities on weeknights until 10:00 p.m. and weekends until midnight). Present your statement to the City Council. Ask if anyone will donate space, old sofas, pool tables, etc. Together, you can start a community coalition (group) to make it happen! Give your coalition a name and contact CADCA (Community Anti-Drug Coalitions of America — www.cadca.org — 1-800-542-2322) for ideas about what you can do as a coalition of teens and adults to create fun free of alcohol and drugs. Do a fundraiser and send a group of teens to the CADCA conference in Washington D.C. in November.

Community Reach-Out Day *submitted by Jeff Yalden*

Why not schedule one day of the year where **everyone** in the school does something to better the community where you live? Have every student volunteer by signing up for his or her choice of community service projects from a list prepared by a student action group. For example, some students might paint an elderly person's house while others may opt to work in a soup kitchen. Some students might volunteer to pick up trash along the town roads and fields while others might plant trees in a nearby park. The idea is to get the **entire** student body involved in improving the community so everyone can take pride in the group's accomplishments. Make certain the local media catches wind of the school's involvement and you're guaranteed a lot of attention. End the day with a barbecue or picnic at a local park to celebrate.

Awesome Ideas for Raising Money, Spirit, AND Awareness!

Mile of Quarters *submitted by Byron V. Garrett*

Inform the student body you are raising a "mile of quarters" for a worthy cause. You want everyone to participate—students, parents, alumni, businesses, and so forth. Work with a local florist and get a mile of ribbon in your school color(s). The ribbon should be wide enough to hold at least four quarters (usually 2-3 inches in width). Select a date, usually a Friday afternoon, to stretch the ribbon on the football field and lay out the quarters. Make sure you give yourself a solid month for the fundraiser. A MILE OF QUARTERS totals more than $10,000, so you can see how a simple idea generates a large sum of money. Key to success—don't accept change other than quarters (you don't want to have to convert the coins). Note: arrange to have a shovel and lots of large buckets to transport the quarters to the bank!

Dollars Under the Bleachers *submitted by Kevin Wanzer*

If your leadership group is raising money for a worthy cause or special event, have a representative talk to the student body in a pep session or assembly about the importance of raising funds. Ask the students to "come together" to help for this one specific reason...right NOW! Have them reach into their pockets and grab a one-dollar bill, then hold it over their heads. At that point, everyone drops a dollar under the bleachers where your group will collect them. This is a quick and effective way to raise a lot of money for a good cause.

Trash-a-thon *submitted by Eric Chester*

Why not kill two birds with one stone by doing something great for your community and raise some cash in the process? Hold a "Trash-a-thon" in which your members pre-solicit pledges on a per-bag basis for the trash they collect in a specific area on a specific day. Local businesses will generally sponsor $5 to $20 for each large lawn and leaf bag of trash collected, while individuals will sponsor people at about 50 cents a bag. Select a real trouble spot for trash and litter, get about 20 or so people to help, blast tunes from a boom box, and take a Saturday morning to beautify your community—and your treasury—simultaneously.

Internet Tutoring for Seniors
submitted by Eric Chester and Craig Hillier

Using your school's computer lab on a Saturday morning, offer internet training for senior citizens where your members serve as the class tutors. Promote your class by posting flyers in senior centers, nursing homes, churches, etc., and/or placing small ads in senior publications. Charge each senior $10 to $20 for a two hour hands-on class where they can learn the basics of going on-line from experienced teen web-surfers. You'll provide a valuable and much-needed service for an often-forgotten segment of your community and raise some serious dollars for your organization in the process!

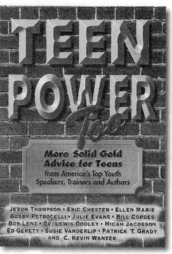